Legendary
Adventures

I will praise thee, O Lord, with my whole heart;
I will show forth all thy marvellous works.

PSALM 9:1

Legendary Adventures

Do you have your own hunting adventures you would like to share?
Please send your stories to:
Pine Creek Publishing
5216 Township Road 118, Baltic, Ohio 43894
and we will begin collecting stories for Volume II.

ISBN-13: 978-0-9792593-0-2
ISBN-10: 0-9792593-0-4

Boone and Crockett Club's score charts are reproduced with
the express written permission of Boone and Crockett Club,
250 Station Dr., Missoula, MT 59801

For additional copies of this book
visit your local bookstore or contact:
Pine Creek Publishing
5216 Township Road 118
Baltic, Ohio 43804

2673 Township Road 421
Sugarcreek, OH 44681

Carlisle Printing
OF WALNUT CREEK Ltd.

Dedication

I WANT TO dedicate this book to God. Without His marvelous creation the book would not have been possible. We could not have captured the priceless memories that we have accumulated over the years. I am grateful to God for His Son Jesus Christ, who gave His life so we can have *everlasting life*. I thank Him for the safety He has granted to us as we have ventured into the outdoors. Repeatedly, He has kept us from harm's way.

I thank my parents for the opportunity to grow up in a Christian home, and for the treasured memories they have brought into my life over the years. They instilled within me, at an early age, an appreciation for God's creation and a love of the outdoors.

Table of Contents

Legendary Adventures

Legendary Adventures

Acknowledgments

COMPILING THIS BOOK, *Legendary Adventures*, has been a great and interesting project for me. When I began collecting hunting stories I was afraid I wouldn't get enough responses to make it worthwhile. Instead, I ended up drawing a line since I went over my goal. Maybe in the future we may be able to add another volume to this one. I know there are more exciting stories out there, so feel free to share your stories. If your story is used, you will receive a free copy of the book.

I want to take the opportunity to thank all of you who contributed stories for this book. Our love of the outdoors has resulted in countless hours close to nature as we have followed our passion for hunting. Our experiences have brought us many wonderful memories which will last a lifetime. I appreciate the effort and time each of you spent writing your story. Without your help this book would not have been possible. I am also grateful to all of you who shared your pictures. A picture says as much as a thousand words and gives the reader a glimpse of the beauty and the story of the outdoors.

I want to thank the staff at Carlisle Printing for their assistance in creating this "adventures" book, which will be enjoyable reading for hunters and nonhunters of all ages.

Finally, a special thank-you to the Boone and Crockett Club for allowing us to share these official score sheets, as well as information which will be a help to readers.

Introduction

HAVE YOU EVER tried to imagine how exciting some adventures would be in reality, like all the stories you have heard or dreamed of trying to experience in the future? Hopefully, in this book you can catch a glimpse of some such adventures, and discover the unpredictability of the wonderful outdoors. My goal is to keep those wonderful adventures and priceless memories alive. I enjoy hearing all kinds of adventure stories and unusual happenings in this awesome hunting world.

Imagine hiking up in high country to hunt those magnificent elk, sitting at the edge of a meadow on a cool morning, staring down into the valley far below with the fog hanging in the lowlands, and all of a sudden hearing the awesome bugle of an elk rising out of a patch of timber. Or feel yourself sitting in a stand in the deep woods of Canada with more mosquitoes buzzing around your head than you have ever laid eyes on before, and trying to score on a black bear. Visualize sneaking along an old logging road in late October trying to stalk a whitetail. When you see movement to your left, you realize the deer has spotted you first. The buck suddenly whirls around and leaves the county. Think about waking up in the middle of the night in a small tent in the wilderness and hearing a lonely coyote howl. Shivers run up your spine ...

That's what I enjoy about being in the great outdoors. There are no limits to the adventures which may lie before you, around the next curve just ahead of you. It is great to take time and get out in an environment where you can spend time to relax and absorb the beauty of God's breathtaking creation.

I think the only way we will succeed is if we spend time outdoors and face reality; learning from our own experience is the way we get on the road that leads to success. I hope all of you enjoy reading this book, and may you experience many more successful adventures in the unknown future.

Let your passion for

adventure and discovery

be matched only by your

thirst for knowledge

and understanding.

In Memory of Grandpa (Henry C. Yoder)

JONAS MAST · Baltic, Ohio

AFTER MY GRANDPA died following a two-month battle with cancer, my grandma showed me this hunting license.

I remember a few years ago, when I told my grandpa that hunting season was here again and that I was looking forward to it, he said, "Ha, one of these days I'll just have to go up on the hill again, and see if I can't get myself a deer, and look at the surprise on some of your faces. I'm sure I could hit one with my 16-gauge shotgun." But he never did.

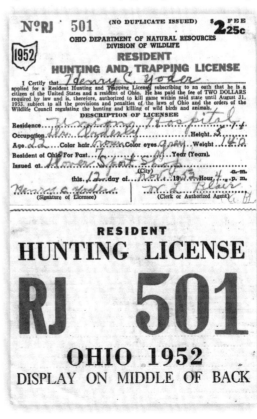

He got this license at Dover Sport Shop on November 12, 1952. He was in residence at Union Hospital where he was a doctor's orderly during his I.W. service from 1952 to

1

1954. For a pastime he and his buddies went carp fishing and gave them to the blacks. One day they fixed their fishing lines and sat back to wait for a strike. When Grandpa's line got a strike, he ran for his catch, stepped into a groundhog hole, and hurt his knee. I think that ended fishing for carp.

Let's stop arguing amongst ourselves about gun, bow, crossbow, with or without bait or dog, or which are the best products to use. We must stick together to be a strong hunting force so we can save our heritage, or it'll be lost forever.

Deer Hunting

MRS. HENRY C. YODER (GRANDMA)

1957 · Geauga County, Ohio

IN 1957 MY husband (Henry C. Yoder) and my brother, Andrew Raber, went to Geauga County to hunt deer, as there were no deer around here in those days. They had no success, but on the way home he bought me a small ceramic doe and fawn set. All these years I have had it on my dresser. It's a nice remembrance, even though Henry never shot a deer.

He also used to hunt rabbits with his little terrier named Patsy. She was pretty good with rabbits. She'd go into the holes, chase out the rabbits, and Henry would shoot them. But it all ended very suddenly. One Sunday evening when we came home, Patsy was gone. We never found out what happened to the dog, but that's when Henry quit hunting rabbits.

If you wonder what they mean—there were no deer around Holmes County years ago. In the year of 1952 the total kill in Ohio was 450 and in 2004 (record high) there were 216,443 killed. The record low was 168 harvested in 1943. Now if we go out and don't see a deer all day we're whining our heads off, so let's count our blessings.

Jonas Mast

Legendary Adventures

Wyoming Antelope Hunt

JONAS MAST · *Baltic, Ohio*

October 2004 · Casper, Wyoming

AFTER BEING SUCCESSFUL in the drawing, four of us headed for Casper, Wyoming. Our hunting party consisted of my brother Jacob, Daniel Yoder, Reuben Nisley, and I.

We left on October 9th at 8:00 A.M. and arrived in Casper at 9:30 the next morning. After a 1,600-mile trip, we were some tired boys. We went to Ron Morrison's place (Thunder Ridge Outfitters). He was our drop camp guide.

We made our camp on Muddy Mountain the next day and scouted for antelope. We saw some nice bucks, including a nice 12". We also saw lots of muley (mule deer) does. When we returned to camp, Jake and Dan said they had seen two nice bull elk fighting about two miles from camp. They said it was pretty awesome.

On October 12th, opening day for antelope hunting, we got out of bed at 6:00 and had a hearty breakfast. We had to drive twelve miles to our hunting ground, an area above Batescreek Ranch where we had seen the nice 12" buck. Daniel saw it again at 10:00 A.M. It had been only 20 yards from him, but he couldn't see it until it ran out. He shot it through the head at a distance of about 200 yards. We had to pack it out about ¾ mile to the truck.

# Legendary Adventures

On the second day we went to another ranch and received permission to hunt. I spotted an antelope about a half mile away on a ridge. I decided to crawl over to a wash and sneak closer to get a shot, and I crawled into a cactus patch! I guess I was focusing too much on the antelope. Anyway, the buck saw me before I got a shot. I suppose he saw me dancing around in pain. My kneecaps looked like a porcupine's back. I tell you what—that was miserable.

I was the last one to get an antelope. I finally saw one running with two does at 200 yards. When they stopped I ranged the distance, but didn't get a reading. However, I decided to aim a little high. I shot and the buck dropped. He got back up, took four steps, and lay down. I shot again, twice, and missed. I went up to Reuben where we finished it off at 200 yards. Later I ranged the distance, and it was 445 yards. I guess I got lucky.

The antelope was not very big, only 8½". But we did get three of our antelope on the second day. I hit mine in the neck with an Encore 7 mm Mag. So much for antelope hunting

did you know?

Mountain lions can live for twelve years in the wild and for up to 25 years in captivity. Males weigh 180-200 pounds, and females weigh 120-140 pounds.

Mule Deer Opening Day

JONAS MAST · Baltic, Ohio

October 2004 · Casper, Wyoming

ON OCTOBER 15, at the dawn of another beautiful day, I sat on top of a ridge to wait until the fog lifted out of the valley below me, because it was new country. Finally the veil lifted, and in one minute visibility went from 5 yards to 300 yards.

I started walking down off the ridge. When I was almost at the bottom, I saw a coyote at about 200 yards. So I lay down to take a shot, but my frame pack bar hit my head and I couldn't shoot. I was trying to take off my frame pack when the coyote spotted me, and the game was over.

I crossed the valley and climbed on top of a bluff about 200 yards from the bottom. For about two hours I was glassing the small pockets on the side of the mountain for muleys. When a buck came running up the bottom, I checked him out, but decided to pass him up. I thought he was only about 18" wide; I forgot that muleys have bigger ears than whitetails.

There was not much going on after that. At about 11:00 Jake two-wayed us and said he had shot a buck. I went over and helped pack it out. It was a nice 2x3 muley. We had to pack it out about ¾ mile. In the evening I went back to the same place on the bluffs. On the way in I saw a herd of does. I spotted a nice big one and settled in. I discovered it was too steep to use bipods where I was located, so I shot offhand at 217 yards and dropped

7

the doe in its tracks.

I went over, cleaned it, and went to get some help, because it was pretty rugged for one person by himself. On the way out I met Jake, and before I got to him, he said, "There goes one behind you." I turned around and saw a nice buck running into the ravine. As he ran up the other side, I prepared. Before he went over the top, he stopped to look around. I ranged it at 150 yards. I shot offhand and hit him in the neck. He crashed into some sagebrush; otherwise he would probably have slid down the slope. It was pretty rough country.

The buck was a nice 3x4, with a 21" spread. On the way out I found six nice (antler) sheds in the bottom. Mule deer hunting is awesome! You have to try it.

For a few weeks each year the leading cause of high blood pressure is the adrenaline rush and inner turmoil that only a legendary hunter himself can identify and prescribe a cure for.

When Farm Boys Head West

ELI MAST · *Wooster, Ohio*

1993 · Gunnison National Forest

MILES BELOW, THE faint bawl of a beef cow broke the stillness of the mid-October mountain air. Closer yet, the raucous caw of a raven and the wind in the pines were music to my ears. Just moments before I had "broken out" of the dark timbered, northeast side of a Colorado ridge, and now I was enjoying a fantastic view of the late fall aspens and a ranch far below. Beyond this first valley, another ridge joined the higher ridges above, and beyond that, snow-covered peaks after snow-covered peaks presented an awesome scene for this Ohio-raised farm boy.

With three inches of fresh snow on the ground, we were looking for mule deer and elk, having backpacked in the day before and set up camp. Two-by-two we had left camp that morning, Levi and Donny, Allen and Leroy, and David and I. Since this was our first adventure into roadless wilderness areas, we thought it best to keep track of each other. (At least one knew where the other was.) This was before GPS units were even heard of ...

David and I had split up around 10:00 A.M. with plans to meet up around noon along this ridge ... and it was now about noon. Still a bit awed by the vastness of the valley to my left, I slowly made my way up the ridge and met up with David.

By this time we had both seen fresh tracks and were eager to follow them. Having made contact again, and established a game plan, we split up once more. David followed his tracks and I pursued the ones I had stumbled upon.

Half an hour later I was easing through dark timber in four to six inches of fresh snow when a glimpse of yellow flashed up ahead. With the 30.06 at the ready, I watched the area for five to ten minutes, when along came a muley buck! With quick strides he made his way down past me. At forty yards an opening appeared in the view of the old Kassner scope, and as the buck's shoulder appeared, I squeezed the trigger. The muley collapsed and skidded to a stop against a two-inch sapling ... down and out.

That was our rookie year of hunting national forests. At 21 to 22 years of age we thought we knew it all but still were keeping our eyes and ears open, just in case there was still anything worthwhile to be learned. Rather fortunately, we had picked Colorado as our destination, having heard from friends that these elk and mule deer tags were "over the counter." (You didn't have to send in applications and depend on a drawing system for tags.)

Other than that we were on our own. We ended up in the town of Gunnison—six of us in a four-door Chevy pickup—looking for tags and a place to hunt elk. We stopped at the first sports store we saw and bought our nonresident tags. The gentleman behind the counter was kind enough to give us directions to a local wilderness area with advice we found quite helpful. Having a cook along would have been nice ... up in the mountains. The person who sold us the tags was willing to send his wife along, if the price was right, but his blushing wife refused.

With new topographic maps of the area, we soon found the trailhead and parked the rig. By this time it was 2:30 P.M. and thunder was rolling around us ... and then it snowed! Another truck and horse trailer rig was parked nearby with a group of hunters waiting for the weather to clear up a bit. They appeared to be your "for real" cowboys, with big wool hats, etc.

The weather cleared up some and we headed up the trail. After the rain and snow the trail was sloppy. Fresh out of the low country, we were soon gasping for oxygen. As mentioned before, this was our first backpacking experience and, well … it showed. None of us had any sturdy frame packs. We were lugging in five-gallon buckets, sleeping bags with handles used as backpacks, a couple day packs with various utilities tied onto the shoulder straps…and I believe the winner was … a suitcase which did a one-way trip to camp. Two of us had light-duty frame packs which we had picked up at the local Wal-Mart as something that *might* come in handy.

I'm sure those cowboys were shaking their heads after we were up the trail and gone. We made it halfway up the first night before darkness caught up with us. After eating eggs and sausage the following morning, we packed up again and continued up the trail. We set up camp in a meadow where we found our first spring and were ready for a seven-day rifle hunt for elk and muleys.

We were fresh out of Ohio and were wary of bears, so everywhere we went we took a rifle along.

The first night it snowed three to four inches. We woke up at night and the tents were sagging in our faces. So we reached up with our hands and bumped the tent to toss off the snow, and it would be okay again for a few more hours. I remember there were three of us in a five-foot by six-foot ridge-type tent. The guy in the middle was okay, but the ones on the outside were generally the ones who woke up with the tent sagging in their faces.

I connected on my muley buck on the first day of hunting, and David also shot a dandy muley buck. We shot our two deer above our camp, a ridge or two apart. By late that evening they were both hung on a newly placed meat pole—just field dressed and skinned—and we had deer steaks and noodles for supper.

We didn't hunt the following day because it was Sunday. With four inches of snow on the ground, we were soon rolling snowballs and building a snowman. One thing led to another and we ended up with a six-foot by eight-foot snow fort! It was about three feet high. Using branches as rafters, and a tarp over the top, we made another shelter with a garbage bag as a door.

The skins of the two mule deer were placed on the snow-covered ground inside the snow fort. A couple "space blankets" on top of the skins, with the sleeping bags on top of that, topped out our sleeping quarters for two of us for the remainder of the hunt. We were just having fun, improvising with what we had.

Needless to say, the boy who had carried in a suitcase was quite tired of it by the time he got to camp (three miles). He had no desire to lug it back out to the trailhead again, so one evening he showed up at the campfire with a sheepish grin and the suitcase … and tossed it on the fire.

We didn't get any elk on that trip, but one of the boys did see a black bear. Other new critters for us were pine martens, porcupines, and golden eagles. Clear at the top of "our mountain" we found the tracks of a mountain lion in two feet of snow! We never saw hide nor hair of the varmint, but his tracks were for real! To us farm country boys this was the final touch needed to convince us that we really were in a wild wilderness area.

We met a few other hunters, but not a whole lot of them, considering the size of the area we were hunting in. From a ridge top one could see a few wall tents of outfitters, miles away. On the pack trails at a lower elevation there were areas where the trail was trampled to a "barnyard slop" by mules and packhorses as they carried gear or meat to and from the trailhead.

At the end of the hunt we left the area behind with considerable regret and stopped in town to thank the gentleman at the sports store for his considerate advice. Of course, we let him know we had connected on two mule deer and were now safely back out again and heading home. By the time we showed up at his store, he had heard of the snow fort up on the mountain used for sleeping quarters and wanted to know if it was ours. Ha! In later years when we would show up at his shop for tags, that was our trademark. "You're the guys who built that snow fort up on the mountain a couple years ago! Welcome back!" He eventually sold the store, and I believe it has now become a rafting place.

The town itself has expanded like everywhere else, with developments and supermarts, but the hunting area has remained virtually unchanged. The wind still howls around the towering rock formations. In the high country the bighorn sheep still travel the ancient trails on the rock ledges. A few years ago two of us even saw a shaggy-haired, white mountain goat!

In the area, we have met locals, as well as folks from Oklahoma, Virginia, Indiana, Vermont, and even Pennsylvania and Tennessee! Besides the mountain goat, bighorn sheep, porcupines, pine martens, mule deer, and elk, we have also seen coyotes, a lynx, a few black bears, a cinnamon-phase black bear, yellow-bellied marmots, weasels, numerous horses and mules, and two white donkeys.

We still hike in to the hunting area; only now we use heavy-duty frame packs—and meat gets packed out the same way. The first year we packed the meat in dry ice for the trip home. Now we take a freezer and a small Honda generator. Our meals have changed from "tin can specials" to "freeze dried" as well, and they are a lot lighter to pack in.

When a fortunate hunter drops an animal in yet another remote corner of the hunting area and we shoulder the meat-laden pack frames for a long haul to the trailhead, we always think, *Next year we're renting horses ... or mules ... or donkeys!* But so far we just never have. Like the ancient saying, "You clean the fish you eat," so we have lugged the meat we downed ... and deep down, loved every minute of it ... and we came back for more.

Legendary Adventures

Opening Morning Surprise

ELMER YODER · *Baltic, Ohio*

November 26, 1990 · Noble County, Ohio

I WILL ALWAYS remember a deer story from the 1990 gun season. I guess you could say it all started on the Friday before the gun season. We were working on a roofing job at Rodhe's IGA store in Millersburg. Right behind the store was a small brushy ravine where some of our crew witnessed a real nice buck service a doe within 75 yards of our vantage point from the new building under construction. I made the remark, "Now isn't that something. I'll hunt all next week and never see a buck like that." Little did I know how wrong I would be.

My brother Bill and I, along with our driver, Laverne Keim, had permission to hunt on a farm in Noble County. We had hunted this place some the previous season and I sort of had my spot picked out. We were there on Monday morning in good time and I followed the trail that led to the back end of the place, about a half mile hike.

There were three ravines which came together at the bottom end like the spokes on a wheel. I went up the hill just a little and sat on the ground, leaning against a large beech tree. I checked the time and it was 20 minutes until legal shooting time, so I relaxed for a while.

About 15 minutes later I heard the distinct sound of a deer walking, but it wasn't light enough to see very well yet. I sure hoped it would hang around a little while yet. About five minutes later I spotted a large deer 40 yards away, so I put the scope on it and saw antlers. He was really gray and was standing in some gray saplings. I really had a tough time seeing him distinctly in the dim light. When I finally was able to see well enough to shoot, I squeezed the trigger on my 20 gauge 870. The buck bounded away at about 30 mph when I shot and took a shortcut through the brush, causing an awful crashing and commotion. Then after one final crash everything was quiet again.

I looked at the time again. It was 7:05 and, since my watch was a few minutes fast, the season was only one minute old when I pulled the trigger. I relaxed for a few minutes, then followed the blood trail for about 80 yards, and found the surprise of my life. There lay a 10-point buck with a 21$^1/_2$" inside spread and a nice heavy rack scoring 130$^+$, and field dressing at 185 pounds.

Laverne had shot at a buck and missed. When he came looking for it, he helped me drag my deer toward Bill's stand as I'd also heard him shoot. We thought he might need help and met him dragging a small 6-pointer. So we helped each other drag out both deer.

Deer Story—2003

ERVIN A. YODER · *Fresno, Ohio*

I TOOK MY bow and some buck lure for deer hunting on the back part of my property in 2003. When I came to the area I had to decide where to sit. I checked the direction of the wind, put out some buck lure, sat back, and waited for a deer.

All of a sudden I saw movement and, looking closely, I saw a deer coming my way. I prepared to shoot as it came a little closer. The deer started to grunt, so I knew he smelled my buck lure. When he stood broadside about 15 yards away, I shot and hit him in the hip. The deer took off and ran down the field with an arrow sticking out of his hip.

I waited a while and then went to see if I could track the deer. I found some blood, but not enough to follow. So I went home.

After waiting at home for two hours I went back again and trailed a little farther, but I still was not able to find enough blood. I went home again and waited until the next morning.

The next day I stationed Henry and Leroy, while Marty and I followed the trail. After about 100 yards I saw some antlers and found my deer, a 10-point buck with a width of 19½ inches and 11-inch tines. With a lot of work we got it home—a nice buck.

Legendary Adventures

My First Deer

ERVIN A. YODER · *Fresno, Ohio*

THE YEAR 1975 was my fourth year of deer hunting. I hunted at Halifax on Raymond Miller's farm. Before I left home my twin brother Mervin said he was going to Walnut Creek to hunt deer.

When I arrived at Halifax I walked back into the woods. To my surprise, there was already somebody at the place I wanted to sit. So I just said, "Hi," and moved on. I knew of another good spot, but there was a hunter sitting there as well. I greeted him and kept on moving.

I picked a third spot and couldn't believe my eyes when I approached. Oh no, there sat my twin brother, Mervin. I said a little more than just hello to him. I was pretty discouraged. Then I went down the railroad track, at the far corner of the Miller farm. I found a place to sit and leaned against a tree.

Sure enough, after 15 minutes I realized something was coming down the woods beside the creek. I was very pleased to see a buck. I don't think my heart was pitter-pattering, but I did feel a little excited. The deer was not quite in my shooting range, so I took my gun and sneaked after it. Okay, here was my chance. I shot. Woops, the deer fell backwards down into the creek.

The shot had not killed the deer. I walked over to it, but instead of shooting again I decided to use my hunting knife and cut its throat and let it bleed to death. Just as I touched the throat, the deer jumped up.

It stumbled over my gun and fell down right beside the weapon. What would I do now? I picked up a stick and threw it at the deer. It got up, moved on a little farther, and lay down again. Since I could get my gun now, I shot the deer again—an 8-point buck.

That is when the work began. I had to drag the deer all the way up to the barn by myself. Nobody else was around. But it didn't really matter. At least I had my first deer. Was it really true? Ha. Ha.

did you know?

The longest tine ever known to have been recorded

for a typical bull elk was 30 7/8" long, scoring 410.

This was an unknown bull picked up in 1948.

Success in Idaho

CRIST NISLEY · *Baltic, Ohio*

September 2003 · Idaho

FROM THE SALTY waters of the Everglades in Florida to the cactus-strewn deserts of Arizona, there is no place that quite touches the heart of an elk hunter in September like the backcountry in the western mountains where you can try to score on one of those magnificent animals with a bow and an elk bugle.

In 2003 I was lucky enough to get an elk tag for Idaho's panhandle Clearwater National Forest. Three of my friends, Sam Beachy, Reuben, Robert, and Dennis Hershberger, were also in our hunting party. When we arrived at our hunting area, we parked the truck at the Kelly Creek bridge. We hiked seven miles up past Twin Peaks to our nice camp spot, with around 65 to 70 pounds in our frame packs. I had been there in 2001, so the trip brought back some good memories.

On the first day of hunting we went to Fern Saddle. By 1:30 we were at a high point where we could glass over towards Junction Mountain. Right away we saw some elk in a little meadow about a half mile below us. So off we went to try out our luck once more.

We set up to do a little elk calling. I was stationed to shoot and Dennis did the calling. On the first bugle a bull bugled right back at us. We called him in, but couldn't get a shot at him because of the thick alders and tules.

I was really excited.

For the next few days we hunted the area with most of our action in the Junction Lake area. We came up with the idea of moving our camp back to Junction Lake, which was about a three-mile hike from where we were camped. Thus we loaded our pack frames once more.

Two bulls bugled on the way over, but we didn't have time to go after them because it was getting dark and raining a little. We got to the lake and had just set up our tents when it really began to snow. We cooked supper and headed for the sleeping bags, being rather tired and glad to have a dry tent.

In the morning when I opened the fly on my tent, the air was foggy with about three inches of snow on the ground. I fired up my little camp stove and melted snow for the water for my coffee and oatmeal, my regular breakfast on this trip.

That evening, just as it was getting dark, I heard an elk bugle off in the distance towards the sunset. Checking our topographic maps in camp that night we tried to calculate the easiest route to the meadow where the bull was bugling. Early the next morning—it was September 15—we had our oatmeal and coffee, loaded our day packs with the grub for the day, and were off once more.

Up on the ridge we bugled to try and locate the elk. When two bulls answered we decided to go for the closest one. We set up and called, but he didn't want to come to us and kept moving away. So we went toward the meadow where we had heard a bull the night before. When we arrived in the area, there were signs of elk everywhere—trails, rubs on the pine trees, and the musky scent of elk.

We bugled but received no answer. We sat down and decided to take a nap and wait until later in the afternoon to try and get the elk fired up. After sitting around for a little while, an elk began to bugle down in a steep ravine. So we set up, with Robert and Dennis about 70 yards in front of me. I was upwind from their position, bugling, raking trees, and snapping branches, trying to sound like another bull intruding his territory.

The bull tolerated the commotion for a while until he had enough. Every time I called he bugled right back at me. The last bugle sounded like he was getting pretty close, and I expected Dennis or Robert would have a shot soon. When I looked out from behind the pine tree where I was calling, the bull elk was strolling through the meadow about 25 yards away. I grabbed my bow, pulled to a full draw, and tried to settle my 30-yard pin on his vitals.

The elk was heading for a little knoll about 30 yards away when I released the arrow. I heard a thud and the bull started running, disappearing behind the knoll. I quickly grabbed my bugle and tried to stop him by bugling. At that very moment I heard some brush cracking and heard him go down, about 30 yards from where I shot him. What a rush of adrenalin I experienced as I walked up to the beautiful animal. He was a nice 5x6 with massive antlers.

Dennis and Robert came running to join the excitement. After all the excitement and high fives it began to dawn on us what hard work was ahead. We were about six miles from the trailhead. We boned out all the meat, put it in game bags, and hung it in a tree until the next morning. Then we all got the frame packs and packed it to the trailhead.

You can very well expect the talk we had in camp that night. Some of the others also had close encounters with bulls but didn't get to notch their tags on any. We also had a raider in camp one evening; he ended up with Robert Hershberger's bear tag. About all that was damaged were two torn-up tents and a dented peanut butter jar.

We experienced all kinds of excitement in our high-country elk camp. Our memories will be cherished for years to come. Till next time, ya'll have some good hunting.

Equipment List: Bear majestic bow, steel force broadheads. Optics: Leica 10x42. Shoes: Rockey Outback. Bugle: "ABE and SONS."

Legendary Adventures

24

Elk Hunting in the Rockies

ABE H. YODER · *Fresno, Ohio*

September 16, 2004 · San Juan National Forest, Colorado

IT WAS SEPTEMBER 16, 2004, and my two brothers, Marvin and David, Robert Hershberger, Ivan Miller, Doran Yoder, and I were camped in the San Juan Mountains of southwest Colorado on a seven-day, self-guided big game muzzleloader hunt. This was day five of our hunt, and as I had already shot a muley buck two days earlier, I was concentrating on filling my bull elk tag. The night before, Robert had said he would like to come with me and call for me, since he had only a muley tag which had been filled the first day of the hunt.

We left the camp on a crisp, clear Rocky Mountain morning and headed for a bowl about two miles out. We called the place Robert's bowl due to some goings-on there a few years earlier, but that's another story! We decided to check Robert's muley kill for bears as I still had an unfilled bear tag in my pocket. Also, the site was right on our route, about a half mile from camp, so not much extra time was needed. Unfortunately, the only visitors at the carcass were some gray jays and about a half dozen coal-black ravens.

With that finished, we headed on a direct course for the bowl which always seemed to have elk. We stopped and called about every 80 to 100 yards. Here is how we'd set up. I would go out front about 30 to 40 yards.

Robert would beat the tar out of a small pine tree and generally just try to sound like an enraged bull ready for a battle! Then he'd bugle a couple times and we would listen for an answering bugle to tell us an elk was near. The third time we set up, Robert did his thing and let out a bugle, when in the clear morning air an answering bugle rang out, punctuated by a roar at the end which can only come from a bull elk. I quickly positioned myself out front while Robert raised some more racket and bugled three more times.

After the third call, the bull elk answered again. He seemed to be circling down below us and, as the air thermals were moving down the mountainside, we knew we had to move, and move fast! I turned to look at Robert, and he was already coming toward me, motioning with his arm. *Run! Let's go!* We took off and barreled down the mountain for approximately 200 yards.

There we set up on top of a small ridge. Robert was on top and I was down over the bank, out of his sight. Robert bugled several times with no answer, so he resorted to cow-calling and crunching twigs to imitate a herd of browsing cows. About ten minutes later I saw the tan body of a moving elk off to my left, and he was closing fast! I checked his rack, saw he was easily legal, raised my 50-caliber Winchester Apex muzzleloader, and waited for him to step into an opening 40 yards away.

As the elk stepped into the opening he stopped broadside and turned his head to stare directly at me. I aimed for the vitals and squeezed the trigger. Kaboom! In a flash he whirled and was gone. Robert came up, all excited, since he didn't even know there was an elk close when I shot.

I didn't feel too confident of my shot placement. For some reason things were rather blurry when I shot. Ha! When we couldn't find any blood on his track I really started getting worried! I was out front looking for blood when Robert said behind me, "Up there he is!"

He had been scanning ahead with binoculars when he spotted the elk's rump about 50 yards up a fairly steep bank. We checked and saw he was down, so I said, "Let's go look at him!" And the race was on.

However, when we came close, the bull elk got halfway up on his front legs, but another shot in the back of his neck quickly subdued him. Even with a shot in the vitals and a bullet in the neck, it was at least five minutes before he quit breathing. I checked my watch and it was 8:05 A.M. Yeehaw!

The bull turned out to be a nice 5x5. At 40 yards I had no idea how big a bull elk actually was. What a fine ending to a beautiful morning.

did you know?

Mountain lions can run at speeds up to 30 mph and make 15-foot vertical leaps, but they have small lungs so they can only run at full speed for a short distance.

Legendary Adventures

The Bear Hunt

DEAN BORNTRAGER · *Millersburg, Ohio*

IT ALL BEGAN early one morning as we were cruising along the road just before dawn, keeping our eyes peeled for a trailhead. We had finally arrived at the land of wide-open spaces, mountains, and best of all, bear country. We were in Rexford, Montana … and had bears in our crosshairs.

On the first morning of our hunt, the trailhead we had been looking for was right up ahead. My friend Jeff and I bailed out of the truck, grabbed our gear, and listened to some last-minute instructions from our guide. "I'll be here to pick you up at dark," he said. We agreed with merely a shake of our heads since the end of the day was the last thing on our minds right now. This was early morning after all, and the day could hold all kinds of possibilities … little did I know.

We started our journey up the mountain. We had quite a ways to hike, but our enthusiasm was high so we soon covered a lot of ground. We planned on hiking to the top of Mt. Robinson. When we reached the top we split up, and I decided to hike back the way we had come until I came to Gold Lake, hoping to see a nice bear somewhere in that vicinity.

"As Gold Lake came into view I looked around for a place to set down my pack and rest. Over to my left I saw a stone wall, so I deposited my gear on the wall, took my binoculars, and began bear scouting.

Around 11:00 A.M. I spotted a bear climbing over a stone wall about two to three miles away. In my excitement I ran pell-mell down the trail to get close to the bear as quickly as possible. I was stopped short, however, by a huge looming figure suddenly appearing in front of me out of nowhere—a cow moose which didn't appreciate my appearance. I believe she thought I was either disrupting her quiet time or was trespassing on her property, because she started barking (yes, you read that right, *barking*) at me. It was a low gruff sound. I guess she must have known that she was bigger than I was and decided to take advantage of the fact by showing me "she was boss."

The moose promptly chased me to the top of the stone wall; my knees were shaking with fright. I moaned inwardly and mentally said good-bye to the bear I had spotted. For a while the cow moose would not let me off the stone wall. She patiently stood in the brush one hundred yards away, guarding me. It was like a game. When I moved, she moved. Finally she got bored harassing this poor hunter and trotted on down the trail, straight towards the area where I had seen the bear. I guess that was her second plan of revenge. She kept on running down the trail and chased up three mule deer bucks which promptly turned around and came running straight toward the stone wall where I was still perched. My guess is she probably said two words, "After him," and they came running for me.

Finally I left my royal perch and went to search for my lost bear. From the first stone wall it had looked like the bear was standing in a clearing, but when I came to my "clearing" it turned out to be an entirely different story. There was brush to my right, brush to my left, brush above, and brush below. You get the point. There was no clearing, just a lot of brush with zero visibility.

When I had first spotted the bear, it had been eating berries, so I began looking for telltale smudges on stones and logs. Finally I found the log where his berry picnic had taken place. I concluded that his stomach had been empty, since he hadn't left any berries for me. I decided to pardon him for his lack of manners.

I had not yet spotted the berry-eating monster the second time, so there was nothing else for me to do but climb another big stone wall. A stone wall can provide an excellent view of an area and enhance wildlife viewing. I scouted for a bit and still wasn't able to catch sight of the bear. Little did I know that all this time he was watching me. I stood on the wall for about ten minutes when my bear decided that his berries just weren't going to hold him over. He decided he needed something bigger, because all of a sudden he jumped down and began the eighty-yard walk to what he thought was going to be a little extra lunch. This walk turned out to be more like a death march.

I still had my gear hanging on my back, because I was not expecting to be stalked by the bear. I had planned on stalking him! The bear stalked right up to the log in front of me. It didn't take me long to drop my extra clothes, grab my gun, and free-hand him right there on the log. I shot the bear at 1:30 P.M. I skinned him right away and left his homely-looking carcass lying right there on the log.

An hour after that deadly shot rang across the mountains, I had skinned the bear and was carrying the head with the rolled-up skin on my back. I began my walk out to the main road, munching on an apple.

It took over four hours to walk back to the trailhead. By that time I was tired and ready to rest. The sun was setting and the evening was beginning to get chilly, so I was glad for the extra clothes I had brought along. I rolled out my bear skin so it could cool off until our guide came back to pick us up. Unloading my gun, I put everything into my fanny pack. My hunting was over for the day. At least, so I thought.

I found a nail and carved my initials and the date into a sandstone which had been marked by earlier travelers as well. Then I lay down and drifted off to sleep.

Some minutes into my nap I awoke to a low growling. Being the kind of guy who doesn't spook easily, I assumed it was my buddy returning and trying to scare me. Lazily blinking my eyes, I suddenly realized that I was terribly mistaken. A mere twelve feet away, and facing me directly, was a hungry, tail-twitching mountain lion! It was like waking up after a bad dream and being relieved that it wasn't true. Only this time I woke up and found reality staring me in the face.

It didn't take me very long to get my eyes wide open and get onto my knees. I yelled, "Get out of here," and waved my hands in what probably looked like a frenzied greeting. I must have appeared a bit scary because he took two leaps backwards.

In the meantime I scrambled for my gun and cartridges. I had unloaded my gun thinking I was done hunting for the day. By this time the hair on my neck were undeniably standing on end! I quickly loaded my gun and stood there waiting to see what the mountain lion had in mind. He looked at me; I looked at him. This was my second staredown of the day. We kept looking at each other for a while, and then for some unknown reason he turned around and trotted down the trail as if he had just been paying me a friendly visit.

I shakily lowered my gun to the ground and wiped the sweat pouring off my face. I thought of visits in my past that had been much more friendly and predictable. The mountain lion, I guess, must have gone in search of some other game. He preferred the kind without a gun.

Five Days of Adventure

JONATHAN BORNTRAGER · *Glenmont, Ohio*

October 21 to 26 · Georgia

MY DAD, MY uncle, my cousin Samuel, and I left for Georgia on a deer hunting trip on October 21, on a Sunday afternoon at about 4:30. The reasons for our hunt were to spend time with my uncle and cousin, shoot a deer with the rifle, and do something different. We drove the rest of the day and most of the next, arriving at the lodge around 5:00 P.M. We unloaded and got settled in, had supper, and hopped into bed.

We were hunting on a 7,000-acre plantation with lots and lots of deer. I saw around 50 deer per day, but most of them were does. I forgot to mention that this whole plantation practiced Quality Deer Management, so any buck that you shot, including a button buck, with less than eight points, or with less than a 14-inch spread inside, cost $550 extra. No *exceptions*. I only saw four bucks, and none of them were shooters, so I just shot a doe. My cousin was the only one who shot a buck. He got it the first day. The second day he could have shot another one if he wouldn't have already filled his tag.

The plantation also had bobcats, quail, wild boars, and coyotes. These were free game. They told us if one of them came along we could shoot. I almost got a shot at a boar, but he was gone too quickly. Dad, Joseph, and Samuel all had a shot at a bobcat. Dad missed, while Joseph and Samuel hit but couldn't find them. Joseph was in a tree stand and his bobcat was facing him at about 20 yards. He shot off one of its legs. We think it was one of the hind legs—about four inches long. He skinned the leg and took it home for a back scratcher. The bobcat was bleeding quite a bit but went into a gopher hole.

Samuel hit his bobcat a little bit too far back and hit the liver and part of the stomach. The cat must have been killed, because he was using the 270 and we found the front half of a partly digested squirrel on the ground. We only hunted for two days, but if we would have had time we would have gone back and dug out Joseph's bobcat. The soil is sandy and it's easy to dig. Joseph was pretty sure he shot right through the vitals. The only reason it didn't drop was because he had a 180 grain bullet and it didn't expand.

I forgot to mention that I did get more than a doe. I shot a coyote the last evening. It came in to about 50 yards and turned broadside. I put a bullet through its vitals and it dropped in its tracks.

We had a lot of fun even though we only got one buck and two does, plus the coyote. There is a different atmosphere in the South. The place where we stayed had about 50 dogs, and the people who worked there shaved once a week, necessary or not. They were very kindhearted, but were laid back.

We hunted in permanent stands every morning and evening with a three-hour break over lunch. There were roads all over the plantation, so they hauled us out to our stands and back again in trucks that were so small and full you couldn't draw a deep breath.

The roadbeds on the plantation were sand … well, actually everything was sand. There was no gravel or concrete on the whole place, because it was so dry and didn't get cold, so they didn't need footers. Their forests were mostly very dense with pines. Also, the land was extremely flat.

In other words, we got exactly what we were looking for—something different.

The plantation is located in Millwood, Georgia

Hunting with the entire family and parent/child hunts are encouraged at the Gopher Plantation.

The main lodge is of log construction that utilized materials and methods common in the late 1800s. This is a showplace of antique furniture and accessories, yet it is accented with the touch of a hunting lodge. A huge fireplace is nestled in a 1,000 sq. ft. great room. Lodging, dining, and entertaining are provided in this spacious relic of the past.

Although the main lodge and all of the cabins are equipped with modern plumbing, this authentic outhouse stands as a reminder of days gone by. This is an example of the meticulous attention to detail which is present throughout the Gopher Plantation.

This typical deer stand is equipped with shutters and curtains for added concealment. The Gopher Plantation has an abundance of stands on its 7,000 acres to provide hunters with fresh areas to hunt that have had limited pressure. Additionally, the portable stands are relocated frequently in order to pattern the changing movement of the deer.

Game Warden Leaves Us with an Impression

PAUL SHETLER · *Charm, Ohio*

1990s

I EXPERIENCED A hunting trip which left a lot of memories back in the 1990s. There was some snow on the ground. I was sneaking through a weed field when a very big buck jumped up. He didn't jump like most deer, but rather just sneaked and trotted. Yes, all that and I didn't shoot. I saw him way down beside another road. Before I knew it, he was coming up the other ridge. By now it was really snowing. The buck was broadside, probably 75 yards away on the other ridge, and I shot twice. He didn't move, so I put my gun on my knee to shoot again.

Well, you guessed it. If you want to jam your gun, this really works! I tried to unjam my gun. The buck started coming over the ridge toward an open field. My son stood watching me with his binoculars. I hollered for him to watch out, and he and the deer both saw each other at the same time, out in the open. The deer had his nose towards the ground like a dog, and Robert turned and shot quickly and missed.

After such a disappointing forenoon we walked approximately one and one-half miles back to the barn for lunch. We began walking cross-country, but the last stretch was on a township road. We were at a curve and I soon said, "Here comes a truck." Robert was on one side of the road and I was on the other, the driver's side. Oh no, it was the game warden. I quickly told him our big buck story.

I could hear Robert unloading his gun (the window was up on that side). Then Robert walked over to my side and I said I had a problem—my gun was loaded. The game warden responded, "It is not as if you were on a highway." He smiled and said, "Good luck," and left. The game warden sure used his common sense, but at the same time left us with a thought for improvement!

did you know?

The largest bighorn ram with the longest horn is 50 7/8" long, and is the longest horn length recorded for a bighorn. It grossed 198 2/8, and had the biggest base of 15 3/8". It was found dead from old age by Colorado D.O.W. in 2005.

Deer Hunting on a Rainy Day

PAUL SHETLER · Charm, Ohio

November 29, 2005

IT WAS RAINING as we traveled with a van 30 miles to the farm where we usually hunted. Like usual, the rest were all packed and ready to go. I packed all my belongings and decided just what corner of the farm was for me.

Oh yes, I thought I'd walk along the road for one-half mile, which was very hilly (my office work keeps me out of shape), until I came to my spot, a nice bowl shape in the woods alongside the road. By now I was wondering why I needed all my clothing.

I came to an old tree stand, so I knew some other hunter also thought this was a good location. Now I sat down several trees from there and thought, *Wow, looks good!* By this time I was tired and sweaty ... and it was still raining. So I took a morning nap.

I don't know what I missed during the first hour, but when I woke up I noticed some movement. I saw a deer shake off the rain. There were two bucks and my scope was fogged over. I tried my binoculars, but by now the deer were behind some trees. I cleaned the scope with my finger, waited until the deer sneaked from behind the tree, aimed at the biggest one, and shot. I hit the buck, then took another shot and hit again. The deer ran 75 yards and flipped over. It was a nice 8-point buck, with a 16¼-inch spread, and 7-inch tines.

Legendary Adventures

Why the Big Ones Get Bigger

PAUL SHETLER · *Charm, Ohio*

December 27, 2005

I WENT WITH my son Ivan to Mary Johns to hunt with a muzzleloader. I told him, "Meet me at 9:00 back there at the bowl, and then we'll hunt together." In the morning there was some snow on the ground. On the way in I saw some deer bedding areas.

When Ivan came we walked out towards the road. I said, "Check these deer beds in the snow." Like a flash, a huge buck moved towards us with big leaps.

I said, "Ivan."

He aimed at the deer about 30 yards from us. When he shot, the buck turned around, and after a few seconds, Ivan said, "Give me your muzzleloader."

Here's what had happened. He had a good open shot, but he hit the hair trigger before the muzzleloader was on the buck.

Talk about sudden excitement and something we'll never forget. The buck probably had a spread of 20 inches or more. As always, the big one gets away. I have never seen a buck running with such quick, long, graceful leaps.

Legendary Adventures

The Fleming County Buck

JONAS MAST · Baltic, Ohio

November 11, 2006 · Fleming County, Kentucky

IT ALL STARTED with a phone call from my buddy, Willis Troyer, from Glenmont. He asked, "Hey, are you interested in going to Kentucky with us for deer hunting? We'd hunt with the bow on Friday and then Saturday is the first day of rifle season."

Well, I couldn't say no 'cause on Wednesday and Thursday I was going to hunt at my cabin in Brinkhaven. On Friday and Saturday we'd be off to Kentucky. Let the hunting begin.

After about three hours of sleep I was picked up at my cabin at 1:45 on Friday morning. We went over to Dennis Raber's place to fetch him yet. We loaded everything into the truck and discovered it was jammed full. The roll-on tarp on the truck bed just barely closed. Well, where were we going to put our deer? We finally decided to go hunting and cross that bridge when we got there.

We stopped at Bob Evans for breakfast, and then we went to Wal-Mart and purchased our licenses and tags. After that we headed for an unknown corner of the universe called Fleming WMA, about 2,200 acres. We arrived around 9:30 A.M., so we grabbed our archery equipment and slung our tree stands on our backs. Off we went in our short-sleeved shirts to make about a mile-and-a-half to two-mile trek up a flat grass bottom which was broken up with some patches of timber.

On each side of the valley was a steep mountainous hillside, heavily wooded with hardwoods. Willis and I decided to go to the back corner to see if we couldn't find some sign of deer, but we found very little. Thus we trekked around some more, climbing up at some pretty steep places. At about 2:30 we decided to settle in for the evening hunt.

While we were walking on the trail we noticed a strong scent of deer glands or a scrape. We dropped to our knees behind a tree and I grunted a few times with my grunt tube. We caught another whiff of scent which almost knocked us over. After a few minutes and no sign of a buck around, we got up, left the area quietly, and set up for the evening.

I hunted about 15 yards from a creek where in some areas nature's carpenter crew was frequently at work, because it was difficult to cross in some places due to beaver dams. I finally crossed the creek on an old cherry log which was sturdy. I was very careful because Dad had always told us boys, "If you get to a beaver dam, never cross on it because you could lose your footing and drown."

I didn't see any deer until after dark when I saw one running through a field. I returned to the truck and asked our drivers, Brandon Yoder and Nathan Otto, if they had seen any.

"I did," Nathan said. "I shot it and pinned it to the ground, but it was only a box turtle."

We all had a good laugh. It was nice to enjoy some humor after a frustrating day. It was too warm, so there wasn't too much action.

We headed for town, found Applebee's, and decided to get some meat there. One guy ordered a steak over easy. We laughed and Nathan said, "Yes ma'am, he wants it sunny side up." She probably thought there was something wrong with him, because he had all his camouflage paint on his arms and face. He was a sight to be seen for sore eyes.

After supper we went to our motel, took nice, long showers, and went to bed so we would have energy to drag out our deer the next day. We were up by 4:45, gathered our stuff, and went to the motel lobby for a continental breakfast. It tasted very good.

After breakfast we headed for the hunting grounds once more, only this time we took rifles—so, deer, you might as well run while you can. We were a little late, because Willis and I had wanted to be in our corner before daylight. To our surprise the place looked like a Wal-Mart parking lot. Oh well, so it goes. We reached a point which seemed favorable because we could see to shoot, so we decided to take our chances there. Maybe we'd even be lucky and see something on the way in.

When we saw a hunter about 50 yards off the trail, we waved at him so he could see us. When we rounded the next bend in the trail, right where we had smelled the deer the previous day, I saw a deer with antlers run up a draw. By the time I got my bearings together and was ready to shoot, the buck stopped about 100 yards up the slope from us. I took about three steps backwards so I could see it. All I could see was his boiler room, but that's all I needed. I raised my trusty Encore 7 mm Mag, put my crosshair on his rib cage, and squeezed the trigger. "Kaboom!" Instantly Willis said, "You got him".

The deer only went about 35 yards and crashed. I tell you what. We covered that 100-yard dash in record time. When we got there we couldn't believe our eyes. To our surprise it was a big 11-point buck with nice tines. We gave a whoop and high fives. Let the party begin!

I told Willis to go on hunting and I would drag the deer out by myself. I looked at my watch; it wasn't 7:30 yet. I gutted the deer and sat there for another two hours. Then I finally decided to begin the 1¼-mile trek with the buck. I met a young hunter at the bottom of the hill who congratulated me. I don't even know his name, but he offered to help me drag my deer. I would never have made it without his help. We spent about two hours until we finally got to the truck. It rained pretty hard most of the way out, so we were very glad to get to the truck and put on some dry clothes.

We talked to a guy who had hunted the area for five years, and he said my buck was the biggest he had seen shot there during that time. I felt pretty fortunate to have been that lucky. I have never worked harder getting a deer out of the woods, so I felt I had earned it. The buck was my first out-of-state whitetail buck and the biggest deer I have shot yet.

That's the end of the Kentucky legend. The inside spread was 17¼ inches and its gross score was 149-6/8. The longest tine was 10 inches.

did you know?

The weight of the largest whitetailed buck ever recorded

in New York was 494 pounds.

Bear Hunting

DAN H. MAST · *Charm, Ohio*

Montana

THIS STORY IS about bear hunting in Montana. We were staying at Rexford with the Charm boys, Eli Yoder, Edward Miller, and Sam Hershberger. We went bow hunting for elk, mule deer, and bears. We did take along a 44 pistol, just in case.

One afternoon Ervin and I went to Stone Hill beside the reservoir where they had seen some bears. Earlier we had hunted in the Cabinet Mountains. Somewhere I drank some water that made me sick, but it didn't affect me for a day or two.

Ervin went ahead of me when we climbed the stone face. I stayed down below and worked my way up to a large stone. I sat down and glassed the other side for bears. After a while I saw a bear on the other side. Even though I felt sick, I stalked the bear and finally came to the place where I had seen it from the rock.

I couldn't see anything, until all of a sudden a bear came running in my direction. I nocked an arrow into my Blackwidow recurve bow. The bear went to my right and I followed him down the mountain. He came to a clearing but was too far away to shoot with the bow. I got out my 44 pistol and fired. The bear sat on his rump and made all kinds of noises. I hit him in the nose and he came running toward me. I fired again when he was only 20 yards away, and then he turned to my left. I shot again and hit him in the hind leg. The bear rolled around and started to chew on his foot. He turned to the right and went running down the hill with me right behind him, blasting some more shots.

The bear went into some tules. You cannot run very fast through them, so I went out around on the outside. When the bear came out on the other side, I finished him off. It was very exciting.

We shot two more bears on that side of Stone Hill.

did you know?

A deer can see 310 degrees without moving its head.

Exciting (But Scary) Elk Hunt

DAN H. MAST · *Charm, Ohio*

THIS STORY IS about elk hunting in the Great Bear across from Glacier National Park. We camped at Grizzly Creek. That sounds a little scary—there actually were grizzlies there. We saw some tracks on the trail on the way in.

The first day we couldn't see or hear any elk. Then the weather turned bad, and it snowed and rained. We finally packed out and went to Rexford again. Along the way we stopped at Eureka to dry our clothes. After that we went to the cabin.

Later on we returned to Glacier and parked the truck at another trailhead. We walked back in to camp. We hunted in pairs. Ervin Yoder and Leroy Yoder were together, while Daniel Frey and I hunted on Elk Ridge. The others went back towards the Humps. We glassed with our binoculars and saw hundreds of elk in Glacier.

Finally we hiked back toward Grizzly Creek where we had hunted before. We just got a glimpse of a bull elk coming out of the Dark Timber area and going back in with a cow. It was too late in the day to go after him. We hiked back to camp, all excited about the next day. We shared our story when the others returned.

We decided to camp there for the night and drive over to Grizzly Creek the next morning. We would hike back to the creek and up to the elk. Yet that night didn't turn out the way I expected. I woke up and heard

49

a strange sound, teeth popping and very serious growling. I grabbed my 44 pistol and was ready to fire. We were sleeping in a tent. I realized Daniel was also awake. I asked him if he had heard the noise. He said he hadn't. We couldn't wake the others, but Daniel and I decided to sleep in the truck. We couldn't sleep very well the rest of the night, but morning finally dawned.

Ervin told us a couple had been killed by a grizzly at the trailhead where we were camping three or four years earlier, so we weren't too sure if we should camp there at all. Looking back, I'd say we were crazy. Just thinking about it makes me shiver.

However, my story is really about elk. We hiked up to the clearing where we saw the bull the day before. We heard Ervin bugle and the bull answered. They were on the other side and could see all the action. When we started bugling, the bull came running and was ready to attack his rival.Daniel was up front and I was 50 to 60 yards down the mountain scraping a tree with a stick. When the bull heard the noise he came running immediately. The elk was running, so Daniel didn't get a good shot and missed. A cow called and the bull stopped. Daniel shot a second time, and this time it was a hit! We tracked the bull even though there was very little blood. Leroy was a little bit behind us when Ervin asked, "Where is Leroy?"

Ervin bugled to alert Leroy of our presence. The bull bugled in response only 70 yards away and came right in. We spread out, and he came within 20 yards of me, but there were too many tules in the way for me to shoot. He caught our scent and left the country.

Elk hunting is like that, similar to turkey hunting, with the turkey gobbling back. Very exciting things can happen out in the wild in the spring and fall.

Respect Bears

DAN H. MAST · *Charm, Ohio*

WE EXPERIENCED A lot of excitement while hunting bears at Sudbury, Ontario, Canada. Marty Quinn was our guide. Our hunting party was from Charm, Ohio: Nelson Beachy, Leroy Yoder, Wayne J. Yoder, Ivan Raber, Marion Yoder, and one other guy who thought he wasn't afraid of bears.

The first evening the guide took three guys back to a power line. Then he told Leroy, Wayne, and me to walk on back from the power line towards a meadow with a pond. We were supposed to wait there until Marion was in position. The guide finally returned. He was going to send me to the stand farthest away because Mr. *me* thought he wasn't afraid of bears. The guide took Wayne and Leroy towards the power line. Some of the baits looked good. Then this little brave guy was supposed to stay at the first stand.

Anyway, when we came back to the first stand the ravens flew away. We also heard another noise that we thought might have been a bear. That's why he didn't send me all the way back. I got on the stand, which was only a platform to sit or stand on. Before sunset I heard a grand sound in the direction of the meadow where we had entered, but I couldn't see anything.

As dusk began to fall, wolves started to howl. The hairs on my neck stood up straight and goose pimples went down my back. The guide had

51

strictly warned us not to move. No bear came in, so I decided to head towards the meadow before dark. I gathered my gear together. When I looked to my left I saw a huge bear come out of the thicket. While he moved away from me I nocked an arrow in my Blackwidow and thought, *I'm gonna get you!*

There were some small pine trees in the meadow. It was time to stalk! I got to the first tree, then to the second. I was not quite close enough yet. There was another tree about 30 yards away from the bear. I started circling around the second tree when the bear stood erect. I thought, *Oh, no! He saw me move.*

He looked like an eight-footer. I kept thinking, *He's gonna get me!* In a second he was on all fours, heading towards me. I froze and the bear passed me like a jet going down a runway. He stopped 40 yards to my right. I thought, *He is looking for me.* It was getting so dark I couldn't see where he went.

I ran as fast as I could! I had to cross a creek about eight or nine feet wide. I cleared it with one jump and ran for the power line just a clipping. I jumped at every twig that cracked. It wouldn't have been so bad if I would have had my noodles together.

When Leroy returned to the truck he said, "What's wrong, Dan?"

"A bear scared me and it's not funny," I said.

He just laughed.

The next night I had a 12-gauge single shot with buckshots, plus the bow. The guide told the others, "I think Dan was scared."

The first night Leroy thought he was gonna scare me when I got to the power line, but it wasn't necessary. A bear had already taken care of that.

On Friday evening I got a bear at the other stand. I could have touched him with my bow if I would have bent over. I respect bears now!

My First Bear Hunt

JOHN SCHLABACH · *Fresno, Ohio*

June 6, 2003 Quebec, Canada

AFTER A FEW rainy days, it was a nice evening to be hunting. I was sitting in a tree stand on top of a rock, about twelve yards from the bear bait, when I saw a bear—my second one on a five-day bear hunt.

Now let me go back to the beginning of our hunt. We left home on June 6, 2003, for our bear hunt in Quebec, Canada, at Balbuzard Outfitters. There were four of us, all first-time bear hunters: Henry Yoder, Reuben Yoder, Aden Yoder, and I. We were pretty excited, because when we arrived we discovered that all twelve hunters who had been there before us that spring had killed a bear.

Our hunt started on Monday, June 9. We only hunted in the evenings, so we didn't always get up very early. They served a light breakfast, then a big lunch and supper (which was usually around 9:00 to 10:00).

Henry shot his bear on the first evening of the hunt, after being on a stand for about 2½ hours. Aden hit one with his bow that evening, but we didn't find it. Our guide went back two days later with a tracking dog and tracked a few miles, but he still didn't find the bear.

On the third day of our hunt the guide took us out just as usual. They like to put their clients on the same stand for three nights in a row. Reuben was dropped off first, about five miles from camp. I was dropped off around eight miles from camp for my stand.

Soon after we were on our stands the bait man came around to put out fresh bait for the bears. Their one bait route was about 80 miles long; the other was 25 miles.

Let's get back to the story. I was sitting on the stand, rather excited because there was a change in the direction of the wind. Sure enough, around 6:10 P.M. I saw a bear come down the trail, but he didn't come in all the way. He turned and left for two hours. The next time I spotted him he was only 20 yards away. This time he came all the way in to the bait. As he put his head into the bucket to eat, I put my scope right above the pail, and as he raised his head I shot him right through the head. He just collapsed right there.

The bear weighed around 180 pounds. We ended up getting one more bear, so we went three for four on our hunt. We all enjoyed our trip very much.

Thanks to the people at Balbuzard and Savage Outfitters.

did you know?

A captive doe in Vermont was almost

20 years old when it died.

54

Seven-Day Elk Hunt

REUBEN MAST · *Charm, Ohio*

September 10-22 · Colorado

WE LEFT TO hunt elk with the bow in Colorado on the 10th of September. We arrived on Monday evening and did some last-minute shopping. We were at the trailhead Tuesday morning at daybreak, after a rough ride on a 40-mile dirt road (took 3½ hours). We had hunted the area before, so we knew where we wanted to set up our camps. There were five hunters, so we set up two camps, one at two miles and the other at five miles. Abe, Duane, and I planned to hunt the lower camp, and Paul and Jr. hunted the upper camp for the first week.

Our camp was set up by 2:00 in the afternoon, so we decided to go hunting in the evening. Duane hadn't hunted the area before, so everything was new for him. We sent him above camp to a meadow where we had seen a lot of elk the previous year. Abe and I didn't have much action, but Duane got a shot at a nice 6x6. The bull elk came out into the meadow to feed with twelve cows and a couple satellite bulls. He missed the first shot, but got a second chance at 52 yards and hit the elk a little too far back. We decided to wait until morning to look for it. We didn't have a good blood trail so it was tough tracking, but we found the elk around noon. After some celebrating, we started packing out meat. The weather was warm so we had to take care of the meat to keep it from spoiling.

On Wednesday morning Paul called in a 5x5 elk but didn't have the best shot, so he didn't go after it until in the afternoon. He didn't find his elk until Thursday morning.

I had shot at a 5x5 at 40 yards on Wednesday evening, but missed. It rained on Thursday night and turned to snow on Friday. By Saturday morning it was 13° with four inches of fresh snow. We had a lot of action but no shots the rest of the week. It warmed up again on Sunday and most of the snow melted. On Monday evening I was hunting the same meadow where Duane shot his elk, and I got a 5x5. Abe helped me debone it and take out one load of meat. I packed out the rest of the meat the next day.

When I returned to camp Abe had hit a 5x5 and needed help tracking, so I ate supper, pretended I wasn't tired, and helped him. We found the elk at midnight, deboned it, and took one load to camp that night. The next morning Jr. went hunting and the rest of us packed out Abe's elk. On Tuesday morning Jr. called in a 5x5 but made a bad shot. We tracked the elk for three miles but never found it.

Our last day of hunting was on Wednesday, so we packed out our camps and headed for home. Even though the hunt was short, we had a lot of fun and action.

did you know?

Between 40-60% of spring-born whitetail doe

fawns will breed in the fall if they are well fed.

"Lost"

LEON WENGERD · Dalton, Ohio

November 1999 · Harrison County, West Virginia

THE WEATHER WAS fair as we made the three-hour trip to West Virginia on a November morning in '99. Steve and I had both hunted a property in Harrison County a few times in the past. In our second year we were hoping for a higher success rate. Located about ten miles across the Ohio River, this area is mostly forested with very few open fields. Hunting was very different from around home where deer have an abundance of forage to choose from.

After we arrived at our destination, Steve dropped me off and headed to his hunting area. We both agreed to hunt until noon and then meet at the road to discuss our plans for the evening hunt.

Right beside the road was a steep incline for half a mile. I headed up a trail which ran parallel with a ridge that in turn connected to the main ridge all the way on top. We had arrived in good time, and I was on my stand before daybreak. We were hoping our timing was right to get some rut action yet, because this was our last time to hunt in West Virginia before the rifle season.

The weather was slightly overcast and time seemed to pass quickly. Everything seemed right for an all-day hunt. With very little action in the forenoon, I thought, *Why not sit all day? Steve would probably understand. In fact, he might even do the same thing.* I made my decision at 11:00 A.M. when a nice buck browsed by 60 yards downhill from me.

In the meantime Steve had shot and wounded a doe but couldn't find it. He wanted me to help look for it, but out of respect he decided to wait until noon rather than spoiling my morning hunt. When I didn't show up at noon, he came up the hill and crossed the ridge to my hunting area. He wasn't too familiar with the area and didn't know exactly where to search for me.

After whistling a few times with no response, he decided to head out to the road and wait a while longer. I had actually heard him and whistled back, but not too loudly for fear of scaring away some deer. After waiting a few minutes without hearing any response, I was relieved and thought now he had gone hunting and wouldn't bother me again.

Out in the truck Steve was getting concerned. He wondered what could have happened that I didn't come out when we had planned. At 2:00 he decided to try to find me, no matter what. This time he whistled more loudly, not concerned about the deer anymore. With no response, a worried Steve headed back to his truck once again. *What now?* he thought. *Leon's probably lost or got hurt somewhere. What if nighttime comes and we still can't find him? Will I have to contact his parents?* Thinking things over, he decided to notify Jimmy, the landowner.

Meanwhile I had heard him again but responded in a similar manner, thinking surely by now he understood I was planning to hunt all day. After he quit whistling, I assumed he went hunting and wouldn't bother me anymore.

When Steve arrived at Jimmy's home (four miles from our hunting area) they discussed the situation and decided to use his ATV to search the woods farther away from the road. None of us (Steve nor I) knew how far it was to the end of the woods.

From my stand I saw an ATV head up a trail a few hundred yards away and across the valley from me. It never occurred to me who it might be.

After a fruitless search, Steve and Jimmy decided they needed to get more people involved. At 4:00 they contacted law enforcement officers and had a search party organized. The police and fire department, plus the local town people, made a sizable group. They spread out and made a big sweep across the hillside.

Around 5:00 I heard lots of commotion on the other side of the ridge. I couldn't understand it, but I finally decided someone probably had shot a deer and other people were helping look for it. All at once I noticed a man come across the ridge and heard him yell. I was so dumbfounded I thought I must have misunderstood. But then I heard him the second time, "Search and rescue! Leon, can you hear me?"

I wasted no time returning his call, making sure there was no question whether I had heard or not. He came down to me and asked if I was all right and not hurt.

Meanwhile, I made preparations for a hasty descent. Concerns about scaring deer were very distant now! Needless to say, I wasn't feeling very proud of my woodsmanship or hunting skills. The man who found me kept asking if I was all right and offered to carry my bow or tree stand. Word soon spread that the "lost" hunter had been found.

We had the opportunity to speak with most of the search party, graciously thanking them for their time and efforts. They slowly dispersed back to their jobs and homes, or whatever they had dropped to come and look for *me*.

It sure makes a person feel humble when so many people drop everything they're doing and come just for you, especially when it could have been avoided if I had abided by my agreement.

A relieved Steve drove back to the motel that night. By the next day we were able to look back and laugh about the experience, but we made sure both of us had a clear understanding when and where we would meet again!

Black Bear from Quebec

JONAS MAST · Baltic, Ohio

June 16, 2006 · Forestville, Quebec, Canada

RAIN WAS DRIPPING down through the trees, a waterfall was roaring down behind me in a ravine, and of all things, clouds of mosquitoes and blackflies were hovering around me just to get their fill. I was just thinking, *How in the world am I supposed to hold still enough in this deep woods of Quebec to get a siting or a shot at a black bear?*

We got a late start on our trip. Galen Coblentz, Roy Yoder, Willis Troyer, and I headed for Forestville, Quebec, at 9:00 P.M. We crossed the border into Canada at 8:30 A.M. the next morning after having a problem getting the guns across. We waited a whole hour at the border. I was the culprit, not that I was an alien or a troublemaker, but I had an Encore muzzleloader. Since you can exchange the barrel with other calibers, the authorities said they needed the serial number of the gun. But muzzleloaders have no serial numbers, so the next time I'll leave mine at home. (We took the guns along in case we didn't get a shot at a bear with a bow.)

After our delay at the border, we followed the St. Lawrence Seaway all the way to Forestville, about 1,100 miles from home. We stopped at a gas station for a break. Roy and I were in line for the restroom when a French person walked up to me and said, "…^ *^…" I said, "Yep," and nodded my head with a smile. So he smiled and was satisfied. I don't know if he asked

61

if we were in line or if we were some stupid Amish.

Our destination was Michal Guy Outfitters in Forestville, Quebec. When we arrived at the lodge, we asked how many bears his clients had gotten.

"Well, let me see," he said. "I think I had 52 hunters and 51 bears this season, with 80% of them taken by bow." Imagine our excitement. Three of us had bows. The lodge had a total of thirteen hunters for the week; the others were from Illinois and Texas.

We had to take all our gear seven miles back to a lake, load it in a boat, and travel about two miles on the lake to our cabin. We were pleased with our cabin. It had hot water, a shower, a toilet, and 12-volt lights. It was pretty nice.

The first night of hunting we all met at the outfitter's cabin at 3:00 P.M. and split up into three groups. Our guide was Jack, an awesome fellow full of energy and willing to do everything it took to get bears for us.

I got to my stand at 4:15. There was a big, loud waterfall behind me, so I knew I would have to rely on my eyes to detect any wildlife. I certainly couldn't hear anything.

I was getting pretty excited, bear hunting in the deep woods (I actually was) with only a bow and a quiver full of arrows with sharp broadheads. If only Mom were here. Ha. Before I left home she said if I get eat'n by a bear it won't be her fault.

I was daydreaming when I spotted movement to my right, or maybe not. What was that? Ah, were my eyes playing tricks again? But no, a bear came sneaking through the brush with no sound at all. Wow! I've got to tell you, I was *very* excited. He came in at 17 yards to the bait site. The bear was very skittish. Finally he tipped the bait bucket and guess what. It was not the first time he did it. He lay down with his butt turned toward me and started to eat up.

I decided, well you better enjoy it as long as you can, you little black critter. After about eight minutes he raised up on his front legs, turned to the left, and exposed his lung for me. I anchored myself for the shot, focused my pin on his lungs right behind the shoulder, and shot. As I released I saw the bear turn, and crack! He left faster than he came. Man, I hit bone somewhere and that little black ball of fur took off like I did something to him.

I sat in the stand and thought about my shot. I finally concluded I had shot him in the shoulder blade and could never expect to find him. I just stayed on my seat. After about twenty minutes I heard a sound in the distance, but I couldn't identify it at first. After hearing it a second time I decided it had to be a death moan; at least it sounded close to the description of others.

I radioed the guide and he arrived in about two minutes. We looked at the bait site and saw some blood. We found an increasing amount of blood as we followed the trail for about 90 yards. Then we lost the trail, so we circled the area, and all at once the guide said, "Hey, Jonas, here he is."

Here is what happened. When the bear got weak he rolled down a slope into a windfall, where he died. The guide looked at the bear, and all he found was a hole in the front left knee. There was no other wound. I guess I got lucky and hit an artery. I was using Spitfire Scorpion broadheads.

We dragged the bear out of the bush and went to the truck to wait for the other guys. About 45 minutes later my hunting partner called and said he shot a nice, big 200+-pound bear. That was Monday night, and by Wednesday night all four of us had bears.

We headed home Thursday noon. At home we found out a tornado had gone through Mt. Hope and Winesburg—that's where our driver lived. Luckily his wife, child, and home were all safe.

So much for black bear hunting.

Legendary Adventures

One Season on the Hershberger Farm

HENRY A. YODER · *Baltic, Ohio*

I GRABBED MY bow and nocked an arrow at ten yards. I drew and released ...

Hunting the Hershberger farm has provided many memories that will never be forgotten. Raymond and I received permission to hunt the farm in 2001. As it turned out, the owner let me build a tepee and do some trapping. Hershberger was a true, friendly old-time farmer, always eager to listen to our stories and adventures.

The first year I hunted I shot my first deer with the bow. Actually, I was lucky enough to take two. After holding out for a buck, and never getting a shot, I settled for a second doe on a cold, snowy January morning.

We hunted the farm for five years until the old farmer moved south, and we could no longer get permission. Little did I know those days would soon be over. Hunting whitetails would never be the same again. My hunting experiences took place in 2003.

Dark clouds hovered overhead. The wind was strong. Just as I reached the tepee, big drops of rain filled the night air. I had planned to run down to the spring for water, but it was too late. I settled down on the inside, wondering if the tepee would keep me dry. It was the first time I used it, and it worked just perfectly.

It seems more often than not I forgot something, whether I was hunting, fishing, or camping. Well, this time I didn't bring an alarm clock. I

65

was sure I'd oversleep, and the next morning was opening day of deer season.

I dozed off, waking up thinking it might be morning. I checked my watch, but it was only ten o'clock! The wind whistled and the rain pattered against the tarp. After sleeping until three o'clock, I decided I'd stay awake the rest of the night until it was time to climb the tree stand! The wind and rain had died down, so I ran to the spring for water. When I returned it began to rain again. I started a fire in the little fireplace in the center of the tepee and made hot dogs and coffee. Checking my watch again, I realized it was six-thirty. After pulling on my hunting clothes and filling my pockets with all the little nickknacks, I grabbed the bow and was out the door.

The wind and rain had not completely died down, but it was very mild. With the wet leaves, walking quietly was no problem. I slipped through the woods, across a pasture, down an old drive through thick brush, and was soon climbing the tree stand. The big old beech tree kept me dry. However, hearing would be a problem with the rain.

Sitting on my perch above the forest floor, I wondered what the day would bring. When movement to the right caught my eye, I took a quick glance. A doe was coming down the well-beaten trail that would bring her within ten yards of my stand. I grabbed my bow and nocked an arrow. At ten yards I drew and released. The shot was low. Missed! She bounded twenty-five yards, quartering away at a sharp angle, never knowing what the sound could have been. Mentally nocking the second arrow, I concentrated on a tuft of hair, drew, and released. The deer spun and fled, but it was too late. The arrow had found its mark and at fifty yards the deer died on the run.

My doe tag was filled ten minutes after the season opened. With only two tags available, I'd hold out for a buck to fill the second tag. But I never got a shot with the bow ... Well, I guess that's not exactly true. I missed once.

Just before dark I grunted on the grunt tube. In response to the call saplings began to shake and out walked the biggest buck I'd seen while bow hunting. It was accompanied by a smaller buck. The smaller one kept me from taking a shot at ten yards. The big buck continued thrashing saplings and kicking up sod. As the bruiser passed by at five yards I drew and released. Missed! The classic mistake. In all the excitement I forgot to pick a spot. The buck trotted off into the woods. Man, was he ever wide! How many points did he have? Probably eight. He didn't have all that many. Yeah, probably eight. Right there he was and I messed up. I doubted if I would ever see him again.

Although I prefer hunting with the bow, with an unfilled tag in my pocket I took my gun off the pegs. I hardly expected to encounter the same buck I had missed previously.

The morning broke with clouds and occasional sunshine. I was cold sitting in the tree stand. Many deer passed safely by my perch. At the end of the day I calculated, and there must have been twenty deer within a hundred yards. But I saw nothing of interest.

The evening fell and I hadn't seen an exceptional buck yet, so I decided to spend the night at the tepee. That hadn't been my plan, and I had no food for the next day. So I divided my lunch, but there wasn't much to divide. The night was cold. Don't get me wrong—it was *very* cold. The next morning everything was frozen. The temperature had dropped down to 13°. It's a good thing I didn't know it at the time or it would have seemed even colder.

The next morning was what I call boring. I simply saw nothing. At noon I decided it was time to look for another location to hunt. I swung my climber onto my back and slowly scouted the farm. Passing my tepee, I headed east to the other end of the woodlot. I saw rubs everywhere; it looked like a decent place to hang a stand. It was 1:30 by the time I got everything in place.

The squirrels were very busy, with lots of gray and some fox squirrels. They entertained me by carrying nuts and chasing each other as if they were playing a game. My mind wandered far from deer hunting, when all of a sudden a rustling in the leaves caught my ear. At a glance I realized what was happening. I saw a nice buck coming at a fast walk, and I knew he would soon be out of sight.

I raised my gun. When the buck paused, I pulled the trigger. The buck dropped in his tracks. I climbed from the tree and walked over to the deer. I counted the points. Never! I counted again. No, this couldn't be true. I counted again, one, two, three. Three points on each side. After convincing myself it had to be true, I grabbed the antlers and pulled, but the deer was so heavy it would not budge. With the help of the old farmer we were able to get him out of the woods.

It was obviously the same buck I had missed earlier with the bow, but then I had thought he was an 8-pointer. He sure looked big walking in the woods. The antlers measured twenty-three inches on the inside, with heavy twenty-four-inch beams, and 10- and 11-inch tines. My buck was a 120 class 6-pointer!

I guess he was the one that got ... didn't get away.

The Second Chance

URA ALLEN ERB · *Glenmont, Ohio*

Opening Day of '04 Gun Season · Glenmont, Ohio

IT WAS A cold and frosty morning on opening day of the 2004 gun season in Ohio. How peaceful it was to sit in a tree stand as the sun came up and hearing all the birds and little critters waking up from a night's sleep. I was daydreaming about the potential for this season, because we'd been seeing some nice bucks in the fields behind our house. It was a blessing to have a hunting ground several hundred yards behind the house.

We sowed the hay field in clover so the deer had their meals in our backyard. Back in the tree stand I saw a buck and three does early in the morning, as well as other deer off and on throughout the forenoon, but didn't get a shot. I heard a lot of shooting around me.

It was about 11:00 when two deer came running through the woods. One stopped broadside at about 80 yards. I shot and dropped it in its tracks. One of my doe tags was now filled. So I thought. When I came to my prey I saw it was a button buck. *Oh no, not a button buck,* were my thoughts, but it was too late.

I started to gut the deer, and while I was gutting I looked up and saw a nice buck coming straight at me. He had no idea I was near. The buck came in to about 70 yards, but he was facing me. I took the shot and hit him. There were blood and hair where he stood, but I couldn't find the deer. I took the button buck home and hung it in the shop.

I returned to my tree stand to try my luck again, to see if a second chance would present itself. At about 3:45 I saw movement out of the corner of my eye. Five does and a small buck were browsing at about 60 yards, beyond some brush. I saw a flash of antlers and, as he emerged from the brush, I saw he was a shooter. I didn't get a shot because he was quartering away from me and wasn't a good target. He went heading down the woods for some other lucky hunter.

By now it was 4:00 and beginning to drizzle. It was getting a little bit miserable. I stayed in my stand because I heard a shot close by. There was light rain by 4:20. Ten minutes later I saw movement ahead of me in the brush. I couldn't believe my eyes. There at 60 yards was the same buck I had seen earlier. I missed the first shot. The deer ran a few yards, then stopped and looked back at me. I shot again, hit him in the neck, and he dropped.

When I left my tree stand to take a look at the buck, he was a bit bigger than I had thought. He had an 8-point frame with 11 scoreable points and an 18½-inch inside spread. The buck scored 146 points gross and netted 139. Thus my deer season didn't turn out too bad after all.

did you know?

Lyme disease spread by deer ticks has

been reported in 49 states.

The Fox and the Gobbler

JOE RABER · *Baltic, Ohio*

April 26, 1999 · Harrison County, Ohio

IT WAS A beautiful spring morning on April 26, 1999, the first day
of turkey season. The evening before I had spotted a big gobbler close to
the cabin which is located only a quarter mile from Clendening Lake.

I settled down in a small sloping ravine. I didn't hear a gobble all morning until around 8:00. Then I heard a turkey warning putt, with flopping
and branches breaking about 70 yards above me. Down the hill came a big
tom with a red fox right behind him. Roughly 30 yards above me the fox
grabbed the tom by his neck and held him down. When I stood up the
fox let him go.

The turkey headed towards me, and the fox, seeing his meal take off,
chased after him again, grabbing him a second time only 20 feet in front
of me. When I moved, the fox ran up the hill. The turkey crawled under
some brush and I finished him off. I was tempted to shoot the fox, which
hung around for awhile, but I thought maybe it had young somewhere. I
didn't want them to starve. Maybe I will get the fox this fall.

The big tom weighed 25 pounds with an 11-inch beard and 1-3/8-inch
spurs. This was the eleventh turkey I have shot since I have been hunting.

Legendary Adventures

Chasing Javelinas in Arizona

JONAS MAST · Baltic, Ohio

January 1-15, 2006 · Alamo Lake, Arizona

IT WAS ANOTHER nice, gorgeous day for January in Arizona. We set up our camp and went scouting along the Santa Maria River bottom. The river was low, so we were able to cross it with our tennis shoes at most places. We hiked over to Cactus Point and saw lots of signs of pigs.

The sides of the river bottoms were grown up with mesquite and salt cedar trees, so at some places if you wanted to cross to the other side of the mountain you had to hike through that brambly mess. You literally had to crawl on hands and knees with a day pack on your back, sometimes for about a quarter mile.

One day we got into a bad mess. In the midst of everything we came to a green water hole with no way around it. We had no idea how deep it was, so we tried to cross it by stepping onto small logs or branches. Everything went well until the last guy in our group made a misstep and, *splash*, he went down to his waist. We were scared at first, but then had a good laugh.

The undergrowth was so thick the beagles at home wouldn't even be able to chase rabbits through such a mess. Anyway, on the way back, as we crossed a ridge, we saw eight pigs cross the river below us. We were a little bit ticked off, but so it goes. We got to camp at 7:30, all tuckered out. We ate supper and went to bed to rest our weary souls (soles). We hiked about fourteen miles of rugged country that day.

We had a nice *Hello* as we got out of our sleeping bags the next morning—it was 29°. At one point I had stepped into the river the day before and the water came over my shoes, so I had to run barefooted over to the wall tent to get a dry pair of socks. After a hearty breakfast, the troop of anxious hunters armed with bows and two-ways were off again.

Crist didn't have much going on, so at noon he came in, got his gun, and went quail hunting. About a mile and a half from camp he came across some pigs and busted them. One ran to about 25 yards, woofing and with its hair on end. To top it off, a small fifteen-pound piggy ran into the brush. Pretty frustrating if you need a bow.

Meanwhile, at 10:00, about three miles downstream, we located the herd we had seen crossing the river the day before. Marvin missed one at about 60 yards, and about half an hour later Willis sent a distress signal for help. The pigs were trying to sneak out the back canyon. Allen and I ran across the gullies to try and meet up with them. I busted them, and all I could do was watch those little miserable critters hightail it for another corner.

The next morning we went upstream and had another wild chase. Marvin radioed me and said there was a pig ready to cross the river about 100 yards above me. I threw off my day pack so I could run faster. I met up with the pig at about 25 yards. When it stopped, I shot, but I hit a twig and missed. It went to the other side of the river where Crist missed three shots and Willis missed one.

Meanwhile, Marvin enjoyed the whole show from the top of a cliff. At the end Crist and Willis were running after the pig to head it off. What a joke—running in a sandy river bottom—and to no avail. The lucky pig got away.

I chased a roadrunner, and I want to say I never saw anything move that fast. No wonder it can outrun the Wily Coyote in the cartoons.

Back in camp we discussed the excitement of chasing the javelinas. One of us remarked that the flies had been circling him during the day. That's when we realized it was Thursday and we hadn't had a shower since the previous Friday. Wow.

Let me say a little more about this gorgeous area. There were saguaro cactus all over the place. They are the ones you see in a lot of national parks with those distinctive arms. It takes about 100 years before the plant starts growing an arm. We often saw some of the biggest ones which had about five arms. Willis had an experience with a jumping cactus one day. He got it on his finger. You can't pull it off, because it will stick to anything. So he had to walk to camp and got one of us with a Leatherman pocketknife to get it off. It was pretty painful.

We had a lot of small washs and little pocket canyons to hunt in. There were also some rugged mountain slopes to hike on. On Old Christmas we didn't hunt. We slept in a little that morning. Then Jack picked us up and we went to Wayside Park, a trailer park at Alamo Lake, about six miles from our camp. We took our weekly shower and ate a nice, hearty meal made back in civilization again.

We planned to walk back to our camp, but there was a guy at the bar who said we were crazy if we did. He gave us a lift instead. It was so funny. He probably had a little too much to drink, because at camp after he dropped us off he must have seen a fairly straight road ahead. Actually there was a two-foot sand ledge on the side, so guess what—he bottomed out his truck. We had to dig away until we got him out. We all had a good laugh.

The next morning Allen and I went to the bluffs, and about a quarter mile from our destination we ran into six pigs. I got a shot at 35 yards, and this little critter stood there with teeth popping and hair all on end. I think he was ticked off that I messed up his breakfast of mesquite beans, but I got no hide nor hair off the little critter.

About 30 minutes later I spotted a gray fox approximately 50 yards away on a ledge below me. I settled my 30-yard pin on him and shot, but the arrow went right over him. He bolted off, but about a minute later he came back and played around a little. I sneaked down to get a closer shot. The fox ran up a little ravine. I sneaked a little closer, to about 26 yards, and I threw a stone just on my side of the ravine. I guess the fox was curious, because he came out of the ravine, sat on top, and watched me at 26 yards. I expected him to run off, but I don't think he knew what a human was. I shot and hit him with a judo point, which was kinda dumb. He ran about 15 yards with me right on his tail, then I lost my footing and landed on my hind end. I broke the ring around my bow sight and suffered some scratches here and there. When I got to the fox, he was chewing on my arrow. He snarled at me, but not for long, because I finished him off before you could say, "Gee whidigers."

Later in the evening Willis and Marvin saw a nice bull elk with some cows. Willis was within 25 yards of the bull at one time. He said it was pretty exciting.

As I sneaked around a bend I heard a *woof-woof* about 30 yards away, and saw another one of those little rascals. Hammer down, the ham's a swingin'. I tell you what. I radioed Crist to station himself and Allen came down a ravine to see if we couldn't get a shot ... all to no avail. The pig went barreling up the steepest part of the point in high gear.

The next morning we went downstream again. Where I was sitting at 9:00, I heard pigs in the salt cedars. About a half hour later I saw them about 70 yards to my left. I began to stalk them up to a point where I could get a 25-yard shot. Everything was going fine until a little draft of wind turned the wrong way and busted them.

About an hour later Willis spotted the pigs where I had been sitting earlier. They came out and rolled in the sand, just like pigs do. Willis took off his chaps, took off his shoes, and stalked them in his stocking feet. He got to within 26 yards and shot. He hit a pig in the shoulder with a muzzy broadhead, and it only went about 30 yards. After that Marvin radioed and said he had also gotten one, about 3½ miles upstream.

That's all the pigs we got. We were two for five. The last day we went quail hunting and shot 22. The last minute Crist went up a canyon yet and found a dead muley. It was a very nice buck, 26 inches wide outside.

We had a good joke on our trip. One day at noon we returned to camp and had a surprise. We found food on our table—two boxes of Rice Krispies, one bowl of raisins, and power bars with some creamy white stuff in the bottom. We figured Jack, our driver, had brought us some treats. Crist and I took some raisins and started chewing. I asked him how they were. With a bewildered look on his face he said, "Well, they are kinda tough." I was wondering if they were for us, because I couldn't chew them.

One Sunday while we played Rook and were hungry for some snacks, 'cause our supplies were kinda low, we ate the two boxes of Rice Krispies for a pastime. After we had eaten almost all of the cereal one of us checked the expiration date. The Rice Krispies were *two years old!* Tell you what. Some boys freaked out.

We asked Jack and Patty about it, and he told us the raisins and stuff were coyote bait. His mom had cleaned out some cabinets and found some old food. After we told him our story, we thought he was going to die from laughing.

Yet in spite of everything, we had a great time.

Legendary Adventures

The Grinnin' Opossum

JONAS MAST · Baltic, Ohio

Holmes County

YOU KNOW THE saying, *grinning like an opossum*. Well, if you don't understand what it means, I'll try to share my experience.

One day early in bow season in '04 we were working in the Columbus area and finished our work early. On the way home brother Jake and I decided to hop off at our hunting grounds and hunt the rest of the afternoon. We had at least five hours of daylight left, so we decided to give it a try.

When we got to the woods I told Jake he could use my hang-on stand in the ravine and I would go about 80 yards up the slope with my Lone Wolf climber. I bid him good luck and ventured on my way to my selected tree by a well-used deer path. Jake's location was super, because there were hardwoods on the slope and deer were always feeding on acorns about an hour and a half before dark.

I settled in. It was about 65° and sunny. After two hours in the stand, I hadn't seen a single movement of deer or any other critters when I heard some leaves rustle down toward Jake's stand. I assumed the deer were starting to feed on acorns, because I heard the noise off and on. It sounded just like a deer walking.

I was searching the far bank with my binoculars, but I couldn't find anything. I thought, *Well, maybe I can't see clearly enough on the other side.* As I sat back and relaxed, I heard the noise again. This time it was closer and I saw movement about 60 yards below me.

As soon as I laid my eye on an opossum, I decided, *You come up here and I'll share some hash with you, you bald-tailed smilin' critter.* Sure enough, he came right up the fencerow. When he got to about 25 yards he was on a log and smiling. *Okay, your time's here, buddy. It's payday.*

I clipped on my release, got into full draw, settled my pin on him, and shot. "Crack." I missed, so I nocked another arrow and shot again. "Crack." Guess what? I missed again. Well, I was about to pull my hair out and was down to one arrow, so I decided to save it for a deer. I sat down and watched this lucky little critter. He stopped and brazenly rested against my arrow, so I suspected he was counting his blessings. I believe I could hear him thinking, *What wush dat, rite behind my nice smooth tail. Well, I'm going to take a sit and rest against this slender branch. Well now, let me see. I think that weird thing up in the tree doesn't look too friendly. Huh, well, I think I'll move on now.*

The opossum sat there for about five minutes against my arrow which was buried rather nicely in a log. He looked at me with a grin and waddled up the woods, just a grinnin' away.

That was all I saw the rest of the afternoon, and Jake didn't see a thing. When I told him my story he began to laugh and said, "Yup, I think he knew what he was grinnin' about."

Well, are you grinnin' like an opossum?

Last-Minute Success

WILLIAM YODER (AGE 15) · *Becks Mills, Ohio*

December 2, 2006 · Spring Mountain, Ohio

ON FRIDAY EVENING after dark, the week of deer gun season, Dad, brother Andrew, and I went to Spring Mountain to hunt the next day. We slept in our camper that night.

On Saturday morning we went to our deer stands. At 25° and windy, it was a bit chilly. I had shot two does with the bow, so I was waiting for a buck. At 9:00 A.M. a little forky came in under my stand, fiddled around a couple minutes, and then continued on his way. At 12:00 I decided to move to a stand down in the hollow to get out of the wind. As I sneaked over the ridge, I spotted a nice buck feeding 40 yards from the stand which I was heading to. He soon disappeared into the thicket.

I climbed into the stand, fastened my safety harness, and settled down for another enjoyable afternoon in the outdoors. At 3:00 P.M. a doe and a button buck meandered past, 15 yards from my stand, feeding on their way. Then at 4:45 P.M. I heard a deer coming out of the thicket. With one glance I saw it was a shooter. He came out at the exact same spot where I had seen him at noon. He came directly toward me, with a tree between us. At 15 yards he stopped, checked out everything, and then turned around and headed back where he had come from. The tree was still in my way so I couldn't shoot. At 20 yards the buck stepped out from behind

81

the tree. One shot from the Thompson Center Omega was all he needed. He crashed within sight of my stand, ten minutes before closing time.

My "last-minute success" was a 10-pointer with a 17¼-inch spread and a gross score of 137-7/8. This was my fifth deer and the first nice buck. Happy hunting and good luck to all of you.

did you know?

Biologists say that antlers of whitetail bucks can grow at

a rate of one-half inch per day during the growing period.

Bear Hunting in Quebec

HARRY YODER · *Glenmont, Ohio*

June 10-14, 2003 · Quebec, Canada

WE PLANNED TO go on our bear hunt with a guy who had a camper, but then we found out that we needed a four-wheel drive vehicle. So we got someone who had a four-wheel drive, but the driver didn't want to hunt bears and we were one hunter short. My sister worked with a girl who said her brother wanted to go hunting with us. That's how we came to pick up this dude none of us had ever met. *This could get ugly*, we thought. At two o'clock in the morning he got into the truck with a gang he had never met.

Danny, our driver, was six feet tall and skinny. Reuben sat in the front seat and gave directions. It seemed like a long time before they got us across the Canadian border, which took extra time because some of us had no photo ID.

We arrived at our motel about six o'clock in the evening and were to meet our guide the next morning at nine. Our guide showed us the location of our tree stands, and luckily Wayne Mast had a GPS or we would have had difficulty finding them again. We were actually glad to have him along, especially in light of the fact that we hadn't known him in the beginning.

We got to our cabin just in time to go bear hunting the first evening.

Willis was dropped off first. His brother was next. We had to go with Wayne to his tree stand because the guide had been attacked by a bear a few days earlier. He wasn't hurt, just very scared. After I was dropped off I found my stand, and the truck went back past after dropping off Wayne Mast.

I was hunting with a longbow with a string tied to my arrow to make tracking a little easier. We had to wear gloves and a head net to keep the mosquitoes away. About an hour before dark a bear approached to about fifteen yards. As I prepared to shoot he took off and ran away. I waited, and about five minutes later he came back, right towards me, and kept on coming until he was directly underneath me. He left again but returned immediately. This time he went to the bait pile, took some of the bait, and dragged it away. I could hear him chomping away at it. About ten minutes later he came back between me and the bait pile and looked away when he was about ten yards from me. I drew my bow, took aim, and shot. My arrow stuck in the ground right underneath him and he took off.

That evening Wayne Troyer and I went fishing yet. We fished right beside our cabin. The lake was small and I don't think there was one fish in it. We could see the bottom with our flashlights and there was nothing there. It was probably twelve-thirty when we retired to bed.

The next morning it was raining when we got up, so we made a big breakfast. After a while the rain quit, so we went fishing. I shot my bow for a while and the others went out on the boats. When it was time for bear hunting, one of the boats had a *dead* trolling motor battery on the other end of the lake. Consequently, we didn't get to our stands until about five o'clock, just a little later than we had planned on. I heard thrushes singing, and a veery let me have a good look at it.

That evening the same little bear came in again, just before dark, and was standing on the bait pile which was on top of a pile of logs. He was fifteen yards away, so I drew my bow, aimed, and shot. I thought it sounded like a hit and the bear took off. My tracking string began coming out. After running ten yards or so he stopped, just stood still for a couple seconds, and then walked away without taking out any tracking string. I waited for the others to come and help me.

When the truck went past to pick up Wayne Mast, I went out to the road to wait. They came back and said a bear had treed Wayne and wouldn't let him come down. So they came and got me. There were three of us: Danny, our driver, Reuben, who had come along just to fish, and I. But we didn't know what to do.

I mentioned going in together because our guide had told us a bear will not usually attack two people. Reuben said there was no way he would go in to the bear. So I looked at Danny and said, "You'll go with me, won't you?"

He didn't say a word. I don't think he wanted to admit that he was scared. I said, "We'll yell and whack on trees, then the bear will think there's a herd of cattle coming." We found a pickax and a shovel and convinced Reuben to shine the spotlight. But he said if the bear comes, he's running the other way.

We went in with Danny and me in the front and Reuben behind us lighting the way, trying to sound like a herd of cattle. Wayne's stand wasn't far from the road, and we weren't far from the stand when Reuben yelled, "There's the bear!"

I thought the bear was going to turn around and run. We could just see his eyes as he turned to get a look as he walked away. Reuben refused to go any farther. I went on in to Wayne. He said he shot an arrow at the bear just to try to scare it away. We decided to search for his arrow, although we were both pretty jittery. We found his arrow with all the feathers chewed up.

We went back to my hunting spot to see if we could find the bear which I had shot. We looked at the place where the bear had stopped about ten yards from where I shot at it. There we found the arrow, but the broadhead wasn't on it anymore. When we looked we found the broadhead stuck in a rotten, wet log. That must have been why it sounded like I hit the bear. Somehow the bear must have gotten the string and arrow tangled in its legs and pulled out the tracking string.

Wayne Troyer hit a bear that evening and we tracked it for quite a ways before we finally gave up.

The next day we went fishing again, and did we ever have fun. We caught 32 pike between 24 and 32 inches.

Our guide was not impressed with our success rate so far. I told him for some reason I was shooting low. He said it might be the result of bending my body when I shot. I was reminded that in practicing at home I had to keep my body straight when shooting from a tree stand.

After we quit fishing we went bear hunting straight from the lake, and of course we were late getting into our stands, like every other evening. Wayne forgot his gloves and ended up with one somehow. The mosquitoes about ate the poor guy alive.

I had missed bears on the first two nights, and now on the third evening I was sitting about fifteen feet up in the same tree. The pine tree provided a very good background and I thought I would have to move quite a bit to be seen. I sat until almost dark, then a bear came from behind the bait pile and walked straight toward me. He turned and started eating the bait, facing in the opposite direction. Once in a while he would stop very nervously and turn his head, watching for danger. One time he looked straight at me. I just froze, hoping he wouldn't see me. It gave me a weird feeling to have a bear stare at me like that.

The bear went on eating, and finally he turned and went around the bait again. He stopped on the other side of the bait pile. All at once I thought of it! *This bear is leaving and, as nervous as he is, he is not coming back.* I didn't know if I could hit him because I had missed the other ones at ten and fifteen yards.

I decided I wouldn't get a better shot, so I drew back my longbow, picked a spot, and shot. This time I remembered to keep my body straight and the arrow flew perfectly. The bear took off, unwinding the tracking string as fast as he could. He had gone about a hundred yards when the tracking string stopped and I heard a loud BAAA! It sounded almost like a calf bawling. Then I knew he must be dead.

I got right on the two-way and told Wayne Mast I thought I had gotten a bear. He said he would be right over. When I went out to the road, he was already there. As I walked around the truck, he was opening the tailgate, and he already had a bear. Wayne hadn't said a word when we talked on the two-way, but now we had two bears.

Before we looked for my bear we decided to pick up the other guys and get some better flashlights. When we picked up Willis, he said he had also hit a bear.

After we found my bear we went and looked for Willis' bear. We found a fairly visible blood trail and were following it when we thought we heard the bear take off. The bear made a circle around us. Finally we couldn't find any more blood and went back to the cabin.

It was about one o'clock in the morning and we still had a lot of pike to clean. Someone made a little bit of supper for us, but Wayne Mast didn't wait for it. He just ate a can of cold pork and beans and went to bed. The rest of us didn't get to bed until two-thirty.

The next morning it was raining while we looked for Willis' bear again, but we just couldn't find it. When we returned Wayne and I skinned our bears and butchered them while the others went fishing.

That evening I went to town with Danny and Reuben and we bought some ice. We also got gasoline. Wayne Mast sat in a tree stand beside Willis that evening and they saw a sow with cubs. He could have shot it, but it was illegal to shoot a bear with cubs.

On Friday evening none of us had any bear hunting action anymore. We had caught a few small trout that morning. Reuben snagged one smaller than his Rapala.

We didn't all get bears, but we had a great deal of excitement and a lot of fun. We also became good friends with Wayne Mast, even though we didn't know him when we left.

My bear weighed roughly 150 pounds (just a guess), and Wayne's bear probably weighed about 90 pounds.

The Last-Minute Buck

DENNIS RABER · *Warsaw, Ohio*

January 31, 2004

ANOTHER DEER SEASON is almost over and I have not filled my last tag. It is January 31, 2004, the last day of deer hunting season. I am in Columbus Children's Hospital with my oldest daughter, Malinda, age 4.

I have not hunted as much as usual this season, for Malinda has leukemia. I spent a lot of days in the hospital. I did not have a lot of time to shoot my compound bow, so I was using my crossbow. I passed up a few small bucks earlier in the season.

Well, it is 12:00 P.M. and the doctor comes in and tells us we can go home. *Great. That way I can go hunting this evening,* I thought.

We were home by 3:00 P.M. I told my wife I was going hunting. She said I'd better. It's my last chance.

I bundled up to keep warm. The temperature was below zero, with snow on the ground. I went over to my friend John. He said he would make a drive for me. He told me where he would sit, so I went way up on the ridge. I was standing there thinking, I *better move 80 yards down the hill.* So I did.

Here I was sitting in a fallen-down treetop, freezing my hind end. I thought to myself, I'd *be happy with a doe.* At 5:15 it was getting colder, with only fifteen minutes left to hunt.

I heard something to my left, and seven does came right for me. A big doe stopped ten yards in front of me. I put my sights on her, then I thought, *That's stupid. What if a buck is following them.* Sure enough. I couldn't believe my eyes. A nice 10-point buck was following the last doe. He came within twenty yards, but I couldn't shoot. The does were on the other side of me, and I was sure they would catch my scent any time. And they did. They took off and so did the buck. When he came, I had very little time to shoot. He leaped over a log and I shot. I saw that I hit him a little behind the vitals.

I went and got the arrow, and was waiting for John ... and shaking a little. Finally John came and we decided to let the buck go for a few hours.

A few hours later John, my brother-in-law Paul, and I went to track the buck. We found the deer, but it took us two hours to drag him out. "So never give up."

The buck scored 146-3/8. Thanks to my friend John.

did you know?

A 12-year-old Kansas whitetail doe was

shot 170 miles from her birthplace.

Trolling up a Trophy Buck

CHRIS LEPLEY · *Mt. Vernon, Ohio* · *written by Dan Long*

Chris Lepley's game plan for taking a record-book whitetail came together perfectly during the 2001 bow season. His secret? Smart scouting, strategic stand placement, and a scent drag that gave him the shot of a lifetime.

HUNTING, STUDYING, AND admiring big deer has been in Chris Lepley's blood for as long as I've known him. So I couldn't have been happier when I heard his message on my voice mail during the fall of 2001.

"Dan, at least 20 scorable points. I killed him. Call me on my cell phone," said the shaken voice.

Chris and I have shared over 20 years as close friends. From junior-high sports to varsity basketball and baseball, a special bond has developed. But not all of it came from our "glory days" at Ohio's Danville High School; in fact, it has strengthened over the recent years from our mutual love of trophy whitetails.

Chris has done everything he can to involve himself with big bucks. From getting a wildlife management degree from Hocking College, to being co-owner of the very popular Pro-Scent deer scents and lure company, to professional videographer and producer of "Close Encounter Whitetails" and "Travelin' For Toms." Partnering with his new outdoor media productions company, Chris doesn't miss a beat. Oh, by the way, he is also a professional whitetail guide on Texas' famous Faith Ranch.

Chris hit his whitetail home run on October 30, 2001, while bow hunting in central Ohio. Here's how he put everything together to take a world-class trophy buck.

Finding the Buck

If you want to be sure you are hunting a great deer, you need proof. Spotting him in late summer, finding his shed in late winter, or even getting a live photo with one of many scouting cameras now available is a great starting point.

"I spend a lot of time driving in late July through mid-August, glassing soybean and alfalfa fields, trying to get a glimpse of a large set of antlers," my friend says of his summer routine. "Once you spot a large buck, then start considering access, permission to hunt, and stand placement."

Many hunters find a beaten-down trail or active rub line and hope to catch a glimpse of a big buck, when a little more time spent in the summer could have helped them narrow down their quest and put them in a position to see one in open season. Unless you can positively identify a trophy buck's presence, you might be spinning your wheels and wasting time.

Low Pressure Scouting

Once you locate a great buck, Chris notes, the last thing you want to do is start trampling through his bedding area. "I knew this particular area that I spotted the buck in well enough to know it had a thick creek bottom that always was full of big rubs and frequent beds," Chris says. "I didn't even scout there (in 2001), because I knew he used it and I didn't want to disturb the area."

The area adjacent to where Chris' buck called home had two family homes within 400 yards, and a township road skirting the property. As long as a world-class whitetail feels no pressure, he will likely remain where he grew up. Even with the lawn mowers, laughing kids, frequent traffic, and the occasional smell of barbecued chicken, this buck stayed right where he'd been in August.

Increased pressure from hunters scouting inside the woods in late summer and early fall can cause a buck to shy away from daytime activity. But when this buck showed up for just 30 seconds on an August afternoon, Chris felt he had a good chance of getting a shot in bow season.

Stand Placement

Chris sets his stands in natural funnels where the predominant winds would blow any human odor away from primary travel corridors. He set up two stands to ambush this buck.

If you're waiting for the right time to enter your hunting area, look for an oncoming storm or heavy rain. Setting your stand during or within 12 hours of inclement weather will help you reduce human scent in the area. Also, be sure to minimize disturbing of the foliage, including cutting wide-open shooting lanes. Wouldn't you notice a new skylight in your living room? So will a big buck.

It was a very windy, rainy day when hunting partner Troy Doup and Chris set up the successful stand. "As I sat in the stand, Troy cleared my shooting lanes with a pull pruner, eliminating the need to touch the limbs with our hands, leaving little to no scent behind," Chris states.

Deer Urine

When hunting big bucks, Chris and I believe that masking our odor with deer urine (buck or doe) is the key to an undetected stand approach. A deer that hears you walking to your stand often will swing downwind to investigate. If you have done a proper job of minimizing your own odor, the deer should be able to smell only the urine, not you. Many times, after entering my stand, I've seen whitetails follow the urine trail right to me.

Chris uses buck urine religiously, and with this buck, it paid off immensely. "I usually spray urine on my boots or a drag," he says. "This time I sprayed urine on the front of my boots and up the shin of the boot. If I walk through high grass, the urine will catch where my boot and pant leg might otherwise spook deer.

"Bucks do weird things when they smell urine," he says. "I've seen bucks of all ages use aggressive behavior such as snort-wheezing, tearing up saplings, and making scrapes when they smell buck urine." Ensuring the use of fresh urine is important. Chris is co-owner of Pro-Scent scents and lures, and guarantees the urine on the shelf is freshly stocked within months or during the current hunting season. Old urine will still work, but fresh works better.

Making the Shot

The magnificent buck was exiting a standing cornfield when he hit the bow hunter's scent trail. Chris saw the entire sequence of events unfold as the deer put his nose to the ground and began to follow the scent. The buck periodically stopped and looked around, but then kept coming, with the wind to his back. He eventually stood just 10 yards from Chris and stared into the woodlot.

As the buck raised his head and executed a lip curl, he noticed a blob of camouflage in a nearby tree. The tree in which Chris was perched was the only one large enough in the vicinity to hold a tree stand with a hunter. The disadvantage to this stand Chris had was that it was too small to break up a human silhouette. Chris, facing the buck with his bowlimb masking the uncovered portion of his face, knew the monster was staring right at him.

Hoping his camouflage had broken up his outline, Chris kept his composure. The buck stared him down for a long time, occasionally lowering his head to smell the ground. Suddenly, some people on the land next door started up their tractor and began to haul more leaves to a pile they were burning. Focusing his attention on the neighbors, the buck wheeled and began walking away from Chris.

Chris was at full draw by the time the buck started to quarter away towards the woods. From 18 yards, Chris' arrow entered the back of the rib cage and lodged in the far shoulder as the deer scampered only 75 yards before falling. The buck made one attempt to get to his feet, but stumbled once again and died. It was then that Chris grabbed his cell phone and started calling friends. He'd just shot the biggest buck he had ever seen alive!

The brute has 21 scorable points and grosses 221 7/8, with a net of 212 5/8 Pope and Young points. The rack's appearance is even more impressive than its score. Most striking are the seven abnormal points, totaling nearly 27 inches, sprouting from the right G-2 tine!

Summary

Many big bucks are shot by sheer luck, especially when the woods are full of hunters and deer are fleeing drives and barrages of gunfire. But as Chris has proven, taking a trophy can be a deliberate process.

Identify a buck's bedding and feeding areas, keep pressure off him when setting up your stands, minimize your odor, and hunt by the wind direction. Follow this formula, and perhaps one day you, too, will be posing with a large antlered mature whitetail.

Legendary Adventures

South African Hunt

ED YODER · *Millersburg, Ohio*

MY DREAM WAS to do more hunting someday and even do some exotic hunts. In 2003 my wife and I were at a sportsmen's show with some friends and met up with some very interesting people that hunt Africa almost every year. After doing some more research, we made a decision to do a hunt with John X Safaris in South Africa, close to the town of Port Elizabeth.

I told my family I will not go unless they will join me, so on May 29, 2005, my wife, daughter, sister-in-law, and I boarded our first plane in Cleveland, Ohio. We flew to Atlanta, got on a huge airbus that holds 585 people, and flew for eight hours before we landed on Syd Island to refuel, which was about halfways. The airline did not allow us to get off the plane, and about an hour later we left with another eight and a half hours of flying. When we arrived in Johannesburg, South Africa, we had gained twelve hours. Can you imagine sitting on a plane for seventeen and a half hours? Our next flight was three and a half hours later to Port Elizabeth. I was glad because I thought we had plenty of time.

Now we had to find our luggage, claim my weapon, and then get in line to prove to the police I was the owner of the firearm. I was given documentation to have filled out and ready (believe me when I tell you they checked out my firearm and ammunition). By the time I was through the checkpoint, I had twenty minutes until boarding time. We had to go approximately 1,000 yards by foot to get to the domestic side of the airport. We found a porter and ran most of the way (now remember, I was carrying my gun and had to check it in at the check-in place there). When we got there I sent the ladies on, and the porter and I went to check in my gun. They told me I need to go and they will send the gun on the next flight. Well, I had heard stories of how this happens. Those guys sell these guns on the street and say they got lost. So not being able to communicate with them other than through the porter, after they had argued for five to ten minutes, I told the porter my family is on the plane and I want him to tell them I will not board this plane without my gun. It is a very special gun to me, because it was given to me by my employees a few years back and I wasn't about to give it up. They sent me back out and said I need to go get a ticket for the next flight which was about an hour or two later.

When I got to the front desk, the porter was talking to the lady and once again I didn't understand a word being said. I saw she had this puzzled look on her face and kept looking out the window. Finally I asked the porter what the problem was. He said she said the plane is still here. Why couldn't they put him on this plane so he could fly with his family? I reached into my pocket and got my wallet out and showed it to her, put it back into my pocket, and told her it would be worth her time. She smiled and the jabber began. They brought the firearm inspector out and went on for another five minutes until I stopped them and said, "Hey, listen, if you guys don't get me and my gun on this flight I will report this to the American officials over at the International side." Immediately she told the inspector to get me on this flight. I slipped the lady $20.00. By now it was departure time, and you guessed it, they held the flight, and within two minutes I was running to my gate with my eyes on the guy carrying my gun. When I got there, the guy asked, "Are you Yoder?" I said, "Yes," and boarded. As I walked down the aisle, everybody gave me a dirty look because of the delay. The doors were closed and we were off to our final destination. Forty-five minutes later we landed and met our guide, Ed Wilson, and made the one-hour drive to camp. All was well. We had all our luggage and my firearm, and the inspector didn't get to sell my gun on the street. After a good dinner we felt like it was bedtime.

The next morning was my first hunting day. But I want to tell you about the day I shot my kudu. We got up early and Joyce wanted to go along that day. Each guide has a tracker and our tracker was Tim Cuse. We had a 30-minute drive to the mountain area where we were going to hunt that day. We arrived just as it was getting daylight. The plan was to drive through the valley and glass the mountains. All of a sudden Ed stopped real quickly and glassed the mountain for the longest ten minutes of my life. Finally I asked Ed, "Do you see one?" There was a kudu about a mile and a half away, and the decision was to go after him. Now we began the long one-and-a-half-mile climb up the mountain. Trust me, this was not easy with rocks the size of a baseball all the way to a football, and millions of them on the steep mountain. Ed sent Tim around, because plans were he would chase the kudu right back where he came from. So Tim left and we were going to wait an hour. Twenty minutes later we saw three more bulls with a herd of eleven cows on the same path. These were more the size we were looking for.

We changed our plan quickly and called Tim on the two-way radio and asked him to stop and wait. We drove around about two and a half miles. Ed thought he knew where the kudu herd was going to run through. We parked the Jeep, and Ed and I made the mile hike up the mountain as Joyce watched from on top of the Jeep. After we walked or ran for a mile, gasping for breath, all of a sudden we spooked the kudu about 100 yards up the hill from where we were. We saw the cows and three bulls run back.

Ed said, "Stop. Let's wait here." We sat there for two hours, waiting and waiting, not sure what all had just happened, when way up on top of the mountain we saw another hunter that looked like he was two inches tall. Ed thought it was another one of his guides and a hunter from our camp out of Texas. He radioed him, and sure enough, it was. Ed explained to me that a large and older kudu will not try to run away. He will back up into a tree and try to wait us out. So Gary, the other guide, glassed the area down towards us and found this kudu bull backed into a tree. All he could see were his horns sticking out past the treetop. He was about 100 yards from us. Gary slowly came our way and finally my kudu bull ran back into an opening. With my Remington 270, I made the shot I was waiting for and put him down. We worked another two hours to get him on the Jeep and headed back to camp to show off my trophy. What a day!

I shot a total of eleven animals: kudu, blue wildebeest, black wildebeest, common blesbuck, white blesbuck, black springbuck, white springbuck, mountain reedbuck, gemsbuck, bushbuck, and an impala. My daughter also shot an impala. We had a total blast and I want to go again soon.

We left the camp and flew to Cape Town to tour for two days. Leaving South Africa with my firearm was quite a challenge too. I and another hunter from Chicago were the last two people on the plane, after telling them a few American ways of doing things. But this time the plane was held up only ten minutes. Once our plane was in the air, and we had leveled out, I saw a guy make his way back, looking at the seat numbers. When he came to my seat he stopped and asked, "Are you Mr. Yoder?"

When I said, "Yes," he said he had been asked to tell me my firearm was on board.

What a relief. We were glad to set foot on American soil, with the rest of our family waiting. Memories, stories, and the shoulder mounts are what we have to tell from this two-week hunting trip to South Africa. I want to repeat the trip again someday.

My First "Adventure" Trip

JONAS MAST · *Baltic, Ohio*

Gunnison, Colorado

AFTER A LONG summer wait and saved, hard-earned dollars, the time had come at last. I was getting pretty excited, because this was the first "adventure" trip for me. I was twenty years old at the time, had spent many restless nights, and had done lots of packing with 80 pounds in a frame pack climbing these Holmes County hills trying to get in shape for the high country.

The night before we left, I tried to get some sleep, but to no avail. There was no sleep to be had, so finally at about 10:00 P.M. I grabbed my pack and slung it on my back. I went for a stroll which ended up being a four-mile-long hike. On the way I talked with some boys who had this bewildered look on their faces, like, is there something wrong with you or what? Well, I got home at about 12:30 A.M., took a shower, went to bed, and slept like a log.

The next morning I was picked up at 6:15, and we were on the road. Our hunting party consisted of Arlen Erb, Jonas Erb, Mike Erb, Merle Coblentz, Bud Ekelberry, our driver, and I. We were off to Colorado.

We spent the night in Lawrence, Kansas, and so far all was going well. But on Tuesday morning when we were going down through the Royal Gorge we hit a snowstorm, and as we came around a curve we ran off the road and stopped against a tree. The only damage was a dent in the bumper, but we had to wait two hours for a wrecker to pull us out. We finally got back on the road again, and we were all grateful that no one had been hurt. We arrived safely in Gunnison that night.

On Wednesday morning we did our last-minute shopping at Wal-Mart. We took our last showers for a week. Then we went to the trailhead and got all our gear in order, packed our frame packs, and began our two-and-a-half-mile hike to our camp, located at an elevation of 9,450 feet above sea level. We had to make two trips, and the altitude gave me a headache. After a lot of uncertainty, we had taken along a wall tent even though we didn't have packhorses. We were very grateful for it.

On Thursday we cut our supply of firewood and made one more trip for food and guns, and then we scouted a little for game. We scouted all day Friday and saw a muley buck, about nine elk, and a spike bull.

Bright and early on Saturday morning we got out of our nice and cozy sleeping bags and ate a hearty breakfast. We prepared for the first day of elk season—it was the second rifle season. Arlen and I went down behind the camp. Arlen got to his spot and I wandered on to the bottom and went to the meadow where we had seen some tracks the day before. I settled in and was ready for action, all the while absorbing the beauty and the new birds and sounds that were awesome so early in the morning. There was not much going on for me, but Arlen missed a mule deer buck. He was the only one who had a muley tag.

In the evening we all returned to camp except Jonas Erb. When he didn't show up for at least an hour, we got a little response with the radio that he was not sure where he was. To signal our location we shot into the air with a rifle, and finally after numerous shots and some confusion he found the camp. We all thought it was a little funny afterwards, because he had felt it was strange that the rest of us guys had a GPS. Well, I guess being prepared pays off.

He said he had a nice 6x6 bull down, but it got away before he got a second shot. So we had a little action the first day of the hunt, and we would wait and see what awaited us on Monday.

Bright and early Monday morning, the dawn of another nice and snowy day, at 6:50 I got to my spot at the edge of a meadow. I nested in a deadfall, so I had a rest for my rifle if I got a shot. I had just relaxed when I heard the crunching of elk running through the frozen snow about 300 yards to my left. I got my rifle ready when I saw two bulls emerge from the timber into the meadow. One was a rag horn and the other a 4x4. When they were about 200 yards from me I whistled, but it didn't stop them. However, they stopped when I hollered. I got the crosshair on the 4x4's vitals and squeezed off a 7 mm round. The bull whirled around and started running back to the timber. I shot offhand at 180 yards, and I noticed the bull was slowing down. As it went behind a spruce tree it began swaying and finally it came crashing down. Of course, I went bailing over the deadfall and cleared the 200-yard dash in record time.

It was hard to grasp that it had actually happened, because it was finally reality instead of a dream. I took the head and went to the camp. On the way I met Arlen and we had high fives. He said he had shot at a bull elk but thought he missed or made a bad shot. We followed it and, after about 100 yards, found it. Thus we had gotten the first two elk. Now is when the work began. I quartered mine and covered it with snow. We got packhorses to take our meat out.

The next evening Merle and I went to the meadow again. Sure enough, about an hour and a half before dark a bull walked out into the meadow at 230 yards. I whistled and he stopped. Merle fired and hit him with a good shot. We ended up shooting about five times before he went down. We gave high fives, quartered the elk, packed it with mine in the snow, and headed for camp. It was dark by the time we got there.

On Wednesday we saw a total of 130 elk, eight spikes and two legal bulls. Jonas Erb went to a meadow to try and intercept them. He wounded one in the leg, but we never found it. In the evening he saw a nice bull at 30 yards, but didn't get a shot. The next morning the three of us with elk packed our antlers out to the van. After that we went for a good five-mile hike in search of a muley for Arlen. We saw three, but no antlers. So we headed for camp again with no luck.

We packed up camp the next day for our trip home. It was not too pleasant. A nice shower would have felt good—it was about a week since our last one—but hey, life's great if you're having fun!

did you know?

The weight of an average three-year-old

Florida Key buck is only 79 pounds.

The Buck That Got Away

MYRON MAST · *Holmesville, Ohio*

Butler, Ohio · Fall 1984

I BOW HUNTED for whitetails the first year I was out of school. Being inexperienced and not having good equipment back then made for some frustrating experiences.

We had some decent hunting on our farm. I worked at a sawmill one-half mile from our place, so I went hunting many an evening after work. Just over the hill from the buildings was a good place to hunt. At a deer crossing one of my brothers had built a tree stand barely eight feet from the ground.

I was hunting on that stand one evening. Coming down the hill to the stand I had squirted some doe-in-heat scent on the heels of my boots. All at once I heard the leaves rattle and a small 8-pointer came tearing down the woods and dashed right up to my stand. He stood there smelling my tree steps, nose straight in the air! Not being high off the ground, I could have reached down and touched him! All at once he whirled around and ran about fifteen yards and stood broadside looking back at me, presenting a nice open shot.

I had drawn my bow when he whirled, and I quickly aimed and let fly. But alas! My arrow flew into the ground close to his hind feet. I figured in my excitement my arrow had fallen off the arrow rest and therefore did not fly true. I was disgusted. It would have been a nice first deer. Better days ahead!

Legendary Adventures

The Special Buck

JOSEPH YODER · *Becks Mills, Ohio*

Spring Mountain, Ohio · October 8, 2005

ON SATURDAY, OCTOBER 8, 2005, the rain clouds kept steadily rolling in. Meanwhile, the north wind kept the temperature hovering around 50°. On this dreary morning my girlfriend, Mary, and I were heading for a two-man ladder tree stand which we had placed close to an apple tree by the edge of our food plot. Some bucks had come there the previous year—the first year we ever hunted on this property.

The property of 70 acres is 95 percent wooded and is surrounded by woods with lots of deer habitat. It is located in the heart of deer country. So the expectations of seeing some deer were pretty high. But you could only hope for a chance at a decent buck.

During the summer we had spent some evenings watching deer from a neighboring field. We saw a lot of deer, but we didn't see any big bucks. With all the good habitat around us, we knew there should be some nice bucks in the area. As we climbed our tree stand, we were unaware that only two hours later we would be hunting from a different location and the biggest buck I ever shot would be lying at our feet.

This year had been a bountiful acorn year, so the deer were not feeding in the hay fields like usual. They were taking advantage of the crop of acorns. They were using different trails to their bedding areas, as we would soon find out.

We got all settled on the tree stand, hoping to see some deer. At daybreak we saw some does at 90 yards downwind. They detected our scent and quickly left. Soon another group of deer came along. They caught our scent, snorted a few times, and left. How disgusting! Well, what is wrong? We are in the wrong spot. So we quickly climbed down and found a spot on the ground on the other side of the trail.

It had been raining off and on all morning, which made the woods dripping wet. The rain was starting to soak through as we wondered if we were just too late. Or if all the deer had smelled us and left. The hunt continued as we constantly scanned our surroundings for any signs of a deer in the area.

Twenty minutes after we left our tree stand, I spotted a buck 40 yards away feeding on acorns while slowly moving in our direction. As he kept coming in the drizzling rain, I checked out those antlers. Yes, I thought I would take him. As I started to make preparations for a shot, my heart rate kept speeding up. The buck kept calmly walking along with no clue of any human presence. While he passed behind a screen of brush, I came to full draw. Now all the practice at the range would be put to the test. As soon as he stepped into the opening at 20 yards, I released an arrow into his vitals. He immediately took off on a dead run down the hill. As he disappeared from our view I heard the fatal crash. He's down! Yes, he's actually down! Wow, what a turn of events! One minute you're getting busted by deer. Twenty minutes later you get a shot at a nice buck.

The buck gross scored 132 with 4 7/8" circumference at the base, 17" inside spread, longest tines were 6 7/8", and field dressed at 190 pounds.

Was I just in the right spot? Or did my Lady Luck have something to do with the turn of events? Well, I sure think it must have had something to do with it. So, guys, if your luck is running low, consider taking that special friend along for a hunt. It just might be your luckiest day.

Elk Hunting in Idaho

ELI A. YODER · *New Bedford, Ohio*

THE SUMMER OF 2006 rolled around. October came and it was time to get ready for Idaho elk hunting again. October 5th found us getting our last-minute things ready. First was our grocery shopping, thinking we had enough for two months instead of two weeks. Next we had to pick up a small enclosed trailer, a wall tent, and a truck cap. Our luck for the day! The cap was six inches too short. Doing some calling on the phone, we found one that fit.

At midnight on Friday morning, October 6, Atlee Yoder, Marty Yoder, Monroe Miller, Daniel Mast, and I started our long ride. First we went to Montana to pick up two of our buddies, Adam Yoder and Aden Miller. We saw enough wild game to keep the days short. We arrived at West Kootenai after 36 hours of driving. It was around noon on Saturday, October 7.

Seeing a lot of good old friends again, and listening to their tall tales and hunting stories, got me all pumped up for the following week.

Monday morning found us loading up Adam's horses and heading for Idaho. It was around noon by the time we left the main road. That meant 24 more miles and three hours of driving. We saw some awesome country and high cliffs. We arrived at our parking spot with shaking knees and pale faces. Now is when the work began! We had to pack up the horses and hike five and a half miles into the backcountry. Having to make two trips with the horses and getting camp set up, everybody was tired and ready for the sleeping bags.

The next morning at five o'clock the alarm woke us up. Our first day of hunting! Everybody had breakfast and we were off to the mountaintops. Already in the first hour I heard Adam shoot. He thought he made a good shot, but couldn't find any blood. Searching most of the day, we had no luck finding his elk. Everybody heard a lot of bugling and saw some elk, but there were no more shots that day.

The second morning at five o'clock everybody was up again, all raring to go. I picked North Creek for the day. Being one and a half miles from camp, I had to get in gear to get up there before daylight. I had hunted only about a mile in from North Creek when I came eye to eye with a nice 6-point bull. Before I could get my gun off the shoulder he took off running, with me boogying after him. I caught him heading up a game trail through some pines. I was quickly trying to pick my shot. When he passed through a little opening, the 300 mag did it again! The elk dropped in his tracks. Doing a couple of tumbles he got caught between two trees. After some spine-tingling death groans, he was down. With some help from Adam we got him turned around so I could gut him.

While I was doing that, there was more action going on. So Adam left, hoping for another bull. Since it was so steep, I couldn't skin the elk where he was. I grabbed him by the antlers and down the mountainside we went, with me guiding him by the antlers. We came to a stop after about 100 yards. We were down in the drainage far enough so I could skin and debone him. With a lot of action in that drainage, Aden and Adam hunted there in the forenoon. They had some close calls but no luck. Adam went after the horse to pack out my elk. Aden said he would come down and help load. He was lucky on the way down and found a nice 6-point rack. It was four-thirty by the time we got to camp. Guess what we had for supper. Some backstraps and liver and onions.

With the rest of the hunters still hearing a lot of bugling, they all had high hopes for bigger bulls than mine. Ha! The third morning I made breakfast for everybody, still grinning from ear to ear. The others all went hunting, but I had a lot of work to do in camp, taking care of my meat and cutting and splitting firewood which was a lot of work. I had to do it with a handsaw.

We were blessed with nice weather so far. In the morning it was in the mid-twenties. By the afternoon when the sun was at its warmest, it was around 50 degrees. I decided it was time for a bath. I fired up the woodstove and went down to the creek and took a bath. Was that ever a jaw-chattering, bone-chilling bath! It didn't take me long to find the fired-up woodstove.

Adam was lucky in the afternoon. He found the bull he had hit the first morning. His shot was a little too far back. I'm guessing he had a little elk fever! We couldn't keep the meat, but he could tag out the antlers (4x5). Everybody had more action, but no more shots. Marty thought he was going to get run over by a derailed freight train before realizing there were some elk coming on the run. But he was in brush so thick that he never got to see them. We had more elk steaks for supper—and some more jaw-chattering baths for the other guys.

The fourth morning found everybody up as usual. They all went hunting except Adam, Atlee, and I. Adam saddled up the horse and went out to the truck to get more horse feed and grub. Atlee and I planned to go out to town. But before we left, Atlee went down to the creek to brush his teeth. Looking up he saw a bull elk watching him. All of a sudden Atlee came running and yelling, "Eli, bull! Eli, bull! Where is your gun?"

I looked up and there was a nice bull. He was about 400 yards away. I quickly grabbed my gun for Atlee, trying to calm him down to make his shot. But with some elk fever, he couldn't make connections. We forgot about going to town and went after the elk instead. We didn't see any more elk the rest of the day. Everybody heard some more bugling again, but no one got an elk. Monroe found a 5-point elk shed. He is pretty good at finding sheds, as he found a whitetail shed the day before.

Day five, and everybody was up and going again. Adam and Marty decided to ride the horses seven miles up to a mountaintop and try to get phone service, just to see if everything was all right at home. This was the first time West for Marty, and he had some eye-popping experiences. Riding up the mountain, they had some narrow paths—places where the trail was only about two feet wide with a 20-foot drop-off. Marty didn't want his horse to slip! He hunted his way back to camp. He had his crosshairs on an elk, but couldn't see if it was a bull or not. Since it was the day before cow season, he couldn't shoot. There were no more elk for the day, and some more chilling baths in the evening.

Day six was Sunday, so we slept in. When we woke up it was raining, and it rained all day. We were kinda spoiled with such nice weather all week. We just sat around camp all day.

On the seventh day it was still raining when we woke up. Yet they all went hunting. Most of them returned to camp by noon, soaking wet. No luck on elk that day.

On the eighth day the plans were to pack out. So Adam and I packed camp together while the others went hunting. It wasn't long before we heard a shot. Daniel thought it had to be Monroe and he was right. Monroe had missed a cow and a calf. Sorry to hear of his bad luck.

Monroe came back to camp all frustrated. Taking a few target shots, he was six inches low at 50 yards. The elk were at 150 yards, so he must have shot underneath them. That's when Monroe told us he slipped on a fallen tree, fell down, and bumped his scope and shins. He said his shins and the missed shots of the elk might heal together.

We had everything packed out by mid-afternoon, and by late evening we were in West Kootenai again.

The next day Daniel and Monroe helped me cut up my elk and pack everything for our long trip home. We saw more wildlife as we traveled, which made the days seem shorter. We came home on October 21st. We all had a good trip! Thanks to everyone for making it a great adventure.

Canadian Big Game Hunt

JOE ERB, ED KLINE, ELI J. YODER · *Charm, Ohio*
Recorded as told to Vernon & Ivan Miller

THE SEEMINGLY ENDLESS stretches of Canadian prairie land made an awesome impression to the foursome traveling westward. Mile after mile the near prefect levelness of this vast area kept their attention. To the motoring companions the prairie expanse was a welcome experience. For them it was not only one of the world's grain bread-baskets, but it was also a connecting corridor from their homeland in the Ohio foothills of the eastern Appalachians to their destination in the western Canadian Rockies.

It was August of 1964 and the four men, Joe Erb an excavator, Aden Miller, a carpenter, Ed Kline, lumber yard employee and Eli Yoder, a lumberman, were heading toward British Columbia on a 14 day guided big game hunt. The four were avid hunters and were traveling in a green and white International Travelall driven by Eli Yoder. The trip's detailed arrangements was finalized with a flip of the coin decision to hunt with Tom Mould, a big game hunter and outfitter in the north central part of British Columbia. The idea to pursue a handful of big game on one trip was an appealing offer during the 1960's; license fees were reasonable, game tags a few dollars and trophy fees were affordable. After game was taken the trophy fee was required on the legal side of hunting.

The seven day trip to Mould's headquarters passed through the north central states into Saskatchewan, Alberta then British Columbia connecting along the eastern border of British Columbia to the Alaskan Highway at Dawson Creek. Beginning at milepost 0 they traveled another 463 miles on this gravel bed road. This was the last leg of the 3000 mile trek west. Entering the Rocky Mountain region the beautiful weather added to the scenic and rugged mountain views. Cumulus clouds floating beyond lofty mountaintops added to the welcome change of scenery. Along the road bends they could now expect wildlife and on one turn came upon a semi rig whose brakes had failed and cut off the road to the left in standing timber rather than crashing along the steeper road grade below.

The long drive ended at Tom Mould's hunting headquarters on the Muncho Lake area of northern British Columbia. Once there some relaxing time was spent around the facility which included fishing on Muncho Lake until the previous hunting party returned. Upon their return and once the pack horses had rested the four began their ride into hunting territory. Aside from the Ohio hunters there were 4 guides and camp help in the party which were met by the cook who had stayed at the main camp from the previous hunt. The pack train consisted of 21 horses all loaded with gear and hunting party. A lunch break along a clear mountain streambed gave the beginning excursion its real dimensions. The hunting urge was real. The men had brought along two 30/06 rifles, a 7mm magnum and a .270 caliber which were in careful protection on the saddle pack scabbards. The .270 was a product of Ed's handiwork as he had skillfully crafted the walnut stock to a Mauser action.

Continuing on toward camp they came upon it later that afternoon in a low lying valley surrounded by lofty mountain peaks towering high above timberline. White canvas hunting tents were staked down that served as sleeping and kitchen facilities. Close by was a stream that provided excellent Artic Grayling fishing which in turn were deliciously prepared by

Nester, the cook. Aside from the meats, steaks and fish Nester did some scrumptious cooking along with baking bread, pies, cakes, and cookies. Camp dining was considered of the best throughout the week.

On their day of hunting they spotted a pair of grizzly bears up ahead. Ed had the pull of the stick for the first shot, so he and Joe set up for a quick shot at 150 yards. On Ed's crack of the gun Joe also shot at the smaller blond colored bear but apparently didn't connect. Ed's grizzly headed for dense thickets and on the steep grade he was last seen rolling down through the brush like a barrel. The guide's decision to pursue the bear the next morning was readily agreed to. The next morning extra precautions were taken. The guide took the lead with the blood trail. He was flanked by Ed and Joe on either side with guns drawn as visibility in the dense thicket was very minimal. Adrenalin was running high with the precarious situation not knowing what to expect; a dead bear or a wounded bear charging at close range. Inching closer the prized grizzly was found dead in the heavy growth and the guides initial response of a miss to Ed's shot was proven otherwise.

Quite soon during the hunt Joe also scored on a grizzly which was also found dead in much the same way the next morning. This one was spotted by Ed while on his horse. The hunters had been warned not to shoot until they had all dismounted and at the moment the last guide was off, Joe connected his shot with the grizzly. On the second shot he went down then stepped into heavy cover on the third shot. The wise decision to leave the wounded grizzly until the next day to avoid conflicts paid off well. Again heading 3 abreast in the cover the stillness suddenly erupted but only to have a bird fly off. Though leaving a healthy scare Ed did soon find the dead bear two steps in front of him.

Not long after staying at the main camp Eli also shot a moose and soon after Ed and Joe were taken to a spike camp another 5 miles off. Being in deep wilderness the hunters were never left alone without a guide on fear of getting lost. The overnight stay going to camp was delayed a couple hours as the horses had wandered off during the night. Even with leg bells and some being hobbled they took some time to round up. The party crossed ridges above timberline and steep mountain trails that the men dismounted and walked along side the horses. They were asked to keep some distance apart so if stones dislodged and began rolling there was less danger of broken bones.

The higher altitude view changed game along with the terrain. Caribou, stone sheep and mountain goats were hunted for. Joe spotted a herd of caribou in a high mountain meadow and with Ed watching from a distant mountain they stalked to within shooting range. Joe's trophy ended up as the 4th largest taken in British Columbia that year. After the caribou was skinned out some meat was left that Ed and his guides hiked back for the next day. While climbing the above ridgeline the white tent of the camp could be seen in the valley floor below and another herd of caribou was spotted. As the trio was sneaking in for the caribou a wolverine suddenly scrambled up a steep stony bank. Taking a quick off-hand shot Ed bagged the hard to find varmint. Then, a few moments later they spotted the caribou from above and he took a good bull. Hunting was at its best and the guides made quick work of skinning out both carcasses.

Meanwhile the other party, Aden and Eli, who had gone the opposite direction from the main camp, was also finding good hunting. They also one day came unexpectedly on a pack of wolves that scattered out. The men's quick shooting downed 2 and wounded another. Eli did get both of them. During the hunt 3 full curl stone sheep were taken. These were high altitude animals. Much time was spent glassing with binoculars and spotting scopes. Once game was spotted a plan was arranged to get within shooting range. On some sunny days after climbing to high points the men took naps while the guides were glassing for game. When Joe's ram was spotted the party began going in the opposite direction then circled around behind the mountain peak. It was noon when they topped the ridge and now as they spotted the sheep down below, the sun would blind the animals keeping them from noticing the approaching hunter. Joe's 30/06 brought down a good trophy stone sheep ram. Ed also made his approach from above coming within 400 yards and he killed a full curl ram. To his astonishment another herd had bedded out of sight closer to the steep grade and at the sound of his shot they slowly walked out in plain sight. It was unreal to see a much bigger ram in this herd.

Back at the main camp Eli had spotted a moose and killed it in view of camp. Later a grizzly was seen coming out of the brush and eating on the carcass. Slipping back into cover it would return to eat a bit later. As Eli pulled the long stick he got the first shot. The guide advised to get closer when the grizzly was feeding and thus were able to get within range. On his first shot he took off running and both Eli and Aden shot again. He stopped before entering a wooded area. They did find a good blood trail and again waited until the following morning to trail him further. Again the drawn gun style tracking was used until they came upon the dead grizzly. The previous day when the cook had set up the spotting scope to see the bear eating, Eli had taken a camera snapshot through the scope and surprisingly it developed well. Both Eli and Aden got a caribou from their spike camp location.

The 14 day hunt was relished greatly by the Ohioans. On the last morning when they were packing up to leave camp one of the guides came to camp and said there is a good sized bull moose on the lake. Joe took off after it and waited until he came out of the water then killed his 52 inch spread mature moose. All in all 2 moose, 4 caribou, 3 stone sheep, 1 mountain goat, 3 grizzlies, 2 wolves and a wolverine were lashed to the pack horses to head out. To the hunter it was interesting to see the guides tie down the packs on the horses. A diamond hitch was used and two men pulled on the rope, often pulling hard enough that the horse would groan.

The party had another interesting day riding back to camp where the horses were corralled, the antlers tied to the outside of the vehicle and were soon ready to say good-by to the well reputed hunting camp. It was also the guides idea that this party had been one of the best hunters they had ever helped guide. It was Ed who seemed to always connect on the first shot and was thereby known by the camp as "One Shot Ed".

Shortly after leaving the Mould headquarters the group stopped for a sandwich at a local restaurant. As they entered another group was having a loud time with drinks at their table and they learned this was the other guide team which they flipped a coin for when deciding which outfitter to hunt with when they were planning the hunting trip back home. The men were thankful for their hospitality and great hunting experience with outfitter Tom Mould. Heading for home on the Alaskan highway they were reminded of what Tom had told them concerning the highway. When the plans were made to build the improved roadway through the northern British Columbia during World War II, Tom was contacted for his ideas on the route for the new highway. With his hunting and trapping experience in the region he did help to establish that part of the route through the Canadian Rockies.

This was undoubtedly one of the best collection of big game trophies to be brought back to Holmes County. Yet today Joe at age 86, Ed at 78 and Eli at 68 talk of the good trip, good hunting and great country to be in. Their companion Aden died 10 years later from a fall during carpentry work.

The Long Hunt

ATLEE YODER · *Rexford, Montana*

I FORGET HOW old I was when I made that first bow, probably four or five years old. The bow consisted of simply a sassafras sapling, chopped to the appropriate length for a little kid, and a piece of baler twine for a string. The arrows were either broken arrows that our dad or older brothers couldn't use and were handed to us, or just some sticks we'd find lying around the shop. We'd cut a notch in one end for a nock.

Back then we were as proud with these simple weapons as other kids are today with their brand-new Mathews bows and a quiver full of carbon arrows. We would tote our bows around and fling arrows at birds and bees, or any creatures that would let us get within bow range. When our bow broke or if we lost it, my brother and I would grab a saw or hatchet and declare war on the sassafras grove. In a few minutes we would have another brand-new bow.

Later, when we were allowed to use some power tools in the shop, we advanced quite a bit in our weapons. We'd save narrow scraps of Plexiglas and tape a stack of them together, whatever we needed for the right poundage.

Then for a while we used those all-fiberglass bows that our dad would pick up at garage sales for a couple bucks.

The first fall after I turned twelve I started hunting whitetails, but it was with a crossbow. I wasn't yet able to cock the bow myself, so an older member of the family would cock it for me at home. Then I'd head for the stand with one shot for the day. Most of my brothers did their deer hunting the first few years this way too. I probably killed four or five deer this way.

My two oldest brothers started shooting compound bows when they were old enough to pull the legal poundage to hunt deer in our state. But my brother, who was two years older than I, started fiddling with home-made bows again, and it didn't take me long to get into it too. These bows were actually shootable, and we switched from crossbows to longbows without going through the compound stage.

A neighbor showed us how to make these bows. They were made out of a tapered piece of ash, with a chunk of wood in the middle for a handle, and then we'd glue a piece of fiberglass on the back and face. Looking back now, I realize these bows were very inaccurate. They stacked like something fierce and had hand shock that made your teeth rattle. But we didn't know any better, so we happily hunted with them.

I remember well the first whitetail buck I killed with a homemade bow and a wooden arrow. I had to lean out over the edge of my tree stand in order to get an arrow past the platform. The deer took off like crazy with part of the shaft and fletching sticking out of his back, and a circle of blood around the shaft. He didn't go far, just out of sight, and then collapsed in a thicket at the base of a telephone pole. That little buck meant a lot more to me than a buck twice his size shot with a compound or crossbow. I was hooked then and there, and I knew if I ever hunted with a modern bow again it would be a long time in coming.

I wish I would have kept track of all the bows I made over the years. Sometimes I would no more than have a bow finished when I'd get the urge to make another one just a little better. Some of them would end up in some exceptionally neat and polished firewood. But gradually they got better.

One I remember better than the others was the first one I made with a wood lamination glued on the face of a limb and up the handle instead of the usual way of having all of the limb on the back of the handle. Christmas was just a few days away and we had company coming to our place. I was quite anxious to have the bow done by then so I could show it off to my cousin. I was mighty proud of the way it was turning out, and I knew that finally this was the Cadillac of all bows. I got it done just in time, the night before Christmas.

The next day we were up in my room. I strung the new bow and was going through a spiel of how good the bow was and why it was so much better than all other bows, and there'd never be another just like it, and so on. Of course my brother and cousin were finding all kinds of flaws and mistakes and said it looked shoddy and probably shot even worse. Well, my brother picked up the bow and started drawing it. He had just reached full draw, when suddenly there was a loud crack and the bow fell to the floor.

I'd heard that sound way too often through the years while testing a new bow for the first time. You always felt like stomping on your hat and beating on the walls when you heard it. This time I froze for a few seconds to let the truth sink in while my cousin roared with delight, but suddenly his trap shut real quickly … when he saw what I did. My brother was holding his wrist with the other hand and there was blood squirting out between his fingers. The whole length of the bottom limb had split and the face lamination snapped up and had sliced through his wrist. We got the blood stopped all right, but he later had to get a doctor to pick fiberglass slivers out of the cut. For the next new bows I made, I wore long leather gloves to test them the first few times.

Like a lot of boys in the eastern states who are limited to only whitetails for big game, I started dreaming of some day hunting elk with a longbow. In the spring of 2001 a bunch of friends who had the same interests as I did got together, and we decided we had talked long enough about going on an elk hunt. It was time to plan a trip and do it. I decided I needed a better bow just for that first bull. I wanted to come up with a different design, so that I could drop down in poundage and still keep my fps up. I had been looking at other longbows and tried to figure out what was needed to make them fast and quiet, and smoother than mine.

So one evening I began making the perfect bow for the hunt of that first elk bull. I drew a new design on a piece of plywood, and erased and changed it a few times until I had the limb shape just the way I wanted it. Then I cut it out and used it for a pattern to make my form for the bow press. I chose brown action wood for the riser block. With zebrawood and some fiber strips, I glued arches in the riser to give it a better appearance. For the limb core I used osage orange and brown action wood for the back and face. I spent many a night in the shop, gluing the riser together, cutting it out, and making sure it fit perfectly inside the bow press. Next came the gluing together of all the bow's laminations. The fun part was adding overlays and cutting the rough shape out. Finally, I sanded it down so the riser grip fit my hand just right.

Then the day came when I could put the string on, tiller it, and then pull it to full draw. I knew right away that this bow would outdo all my other bows by a far cry. It pulled 55 pounds and shot arrows faster than the last bow I had made that pulled 65 pounds. So you can probably understand why I was considerably impressed by the time I had all the fine sanding done and put a few coats of finish on it to keep the moisture out.

The first week in September found four of us boys hiking in the Clearwater National Forest in Idaho with longbows and recurves. There had been eight of us altogether. We had decided on two different trailheads about six miles apart. The four of us had been dropped off at our trailhead while the other four had driven off to theirs. We would be hunting elk and bears with bows for fifteen days. The four of us made camp beside a cold mountain spring seven miles back in.

We each had our own little tent to sleep in, then we had a tarp strung up beside the cooking fire in case we got nasty weather. We had some awesome weather those next fifteen days. We had lots of game around us, but for some eastern rookies in an unknown area to connect with an elk bull was gonna take a lot of luck.

We saw game every day and had some close encounters with both bears and elk, but nobody took any shots. Although we didn't bring any meat home on that trip, it will go down as one of my best hunts. It seems like it's always more exciting the first time you try something new, and you'll remember it better.

The first western hunting trip was the beginning of many more to come for most of us in the group. I crossed to the east side of the Mississippi knowing good and well that the hunt for that first bull hadn't come to an end yet.

The following spring my brother, a friend, and I decided we'd dig in a little deeper. We planned to move to a small Amish community in northwestern Montana for the summer, then by fall archery season we'd be able to buy resident hunting licenses. We would hit the hunting season good and hard that fall before returning to our home state of Ohio.

That summer found us batchin' in some small shacks without any plumbing, but I guess we did have running water—if we let it run from a five-gallon bucket to the sink.

We soon had a nice shower set up on the back porch. We poked a bunch of holes in the bottom of a five-gallon bucket. All a fella had to do was hang it on a nail above his head, pour it full of warm water, and stand underneath. For awhile in the spring we had to stand on a chunk of ice that had frozen on the deck under the eave. You can be sure we didn't take any showers just for kicks those days.

During the summer we made sure we did our share of hiking and camping, and all the while keeping our eyes peeled for elk sign. September finally rolled around, but we hadn't found any real promising spots. We'd end up still trying to locate elk.

The third week in September finally brought some excitement. Lester came to camp one night, and said he heard a bull going strong down in a deep drainage just before dark. The next morning it was raining cats and dogs, but when it let up late in the morning we headed for that drainage where Lester had heard the bull. We got the bull going all right but couldn't get him to budge. We decided to go back out and glass for bears through the hot part of the day. Late in the afternoon we returned and hammered away on the bull. We finally moved in pretty close and, sure enough, had him fired up, but then it got dark on us.

The next morning from the top of the ridge we heard the elk bugling down in the same hole again. And a hole it was indeed. That drainage was so overgrown with alders and shin whackers that if a fellow was lucky he could find a path to crawl through, but a lot of places you simply had to back out again.

Well, we didn't get the bull that day or the next, or the next, even though he was bugling in the same place every day. Usually he'd answer our calls until we got within a few hundred yards of him, and then he'd shut up on us. Not knowing where he was for sure, and the fear of spooking him, caused us to back out again.

One morning after he'd quit us again we were walking up an old logging road when we accidentally walked up on him. He wasn't more than 20 yards beside us, giving a small sapling hash with his six-point rack. We both nocked arrows and froze in our tracks. The bull never knew we were there, but all we could see were some long ivory tines and patches of tan hair through the brush. Suddenly he turned and walked back into the jungle and disappeared.

Day after day we played cat and mouse games with the same bull in the same drainage. I told Lester a bull that stays in the same hole and outwits us day after day oughta have a name. So for some silly reason we named him *Mervin*.

One day we approached in on the bull from the opposite side of the creek. Lester was giving *Mervin* bugle for bugle and crashing around the brush like a crazed bull, and I was staying ahead 20 to 40 yards, sounding like the sweetest little cow a bull could ever want.

Just like usual, *Mervin* wouldn't budge an inch. But at least he kept talking this time. Finally we were past the few hundred yard mark where he always became quiet, so we realized the fella was serious this time. He wasn't bugling at us anymore. He was screaming, roaring, and bellowing like a domestic bull. We could hear him raking trees and slapping around in a wallow, but still he stood his ground.

We'd call from one position for awhile, then move in a little closer. Sometimes we'd have to crawl on hands and knees through the brush. Next we would walk on blowdowns above the mess and kept our fingers crossed, just hoping *Mervin* wouldn't charge in while we were in such a position.

Suddenly I heard brush cracking right in front of me and alders swaying from side to side. Right there I knew old *Mervin* made his mistake. He was coming in straight for me. I tightened my grip on the bow, extended my bow arm, and put tension on the string. By this time I could see four dark legs coming my way. The bull would be at five paces before we would be able to see each other because of the brush, and I wanted to be ready when that happened. Suddenly, there he was, but something was wrong. There was no wide-spread six-point rack on his head. There was nothing there, I mean nothing. It was a she. A stupid cow had walked in on us. My tensed body relaxed and the broadhead on the end of my arrow quit jumping around—stupid broadheads anyway. The cow nibbled on some leaves, then slowly kept coming toward me. Finally she was standing no more than an arrow length in front of my broadhead. When she turned her head to nibble on some leaves, just to see if I could, I pulled my bow to full draw then slowly let forward again. She never saw it, but soon she kinda figured out something wasn't quite right, turned, and went crashing through the brush.

For a while I thought all was lost. Then behind me Lester whipped out his bugle and told the world that he was handling this show. Whoever was up ahead had better be making tracks for some other territory or else! *Mervin* answered with a scream and told us he was king of all kings, and if we as much as made one step he'd come and cut us to ribbons and scatter us for the ravens. I turned around and grinned at Lester and he gave me the thumbs up. The game was still on.

We got together and in whispers decided that the reason the bull wasn't coming to us was because of the little gully between us and him. We'd have to work past him on our side, then cross over above him, to keep the thermal in our favor.

Lester and the bull screamed and threatened a few more times, and then we started moving. I was ahead of Lester, walking over a blowdown about six feet off the ground, when things started happening. There was crashing and popping, and from my perch I realized *Mervin* was charging in at the worst time and place. I saw Lester step off his end of the log and disappear. I took one glance at the jungle of shin whackers below and then crashed in amongst them.

From my nest I saw twelve ivory points laid back over the bull's back come crashing toward Lester's position. Then he stopped. Everything got deathly quiet. I saw the rack swing my way, then toward Lester, then my way again, and back again. He had us pinned down, and trying to thread an arrow through the brush would have been hopeless.

Here he had been hearing all this screaming, crashing, and bellowing just minutes before. Now when he came in to carry out his threats, he couldn't find another bull and not a peep either. It didn't take the bull long to figure out something wasn't quite right and those two-legged critters probably had something to do with it. There was a crashing and pounding of hoofs going the other way and then the woods quieted down.

By this time my heart had fallen down to my toenails, and when my partner poked his head over a blowdown, by the look on his face I saw that he had lost his down among his shoes as well. For five and a half hours we had been working that bull, and finally got him in. Then we up and blew it. I felt like wrapping my silly bow around a tree trunk and smashing my hat. But then I decided if that got us anywhere it would be in the wrong place anyway. So I just beat on a tree with a stick.

After we had discussed all the ifs and buts, we dragged our weary bodies out of the ravine and headed for camp. From then on, my second bow season for that first-tradition bull tapered off and I was elk-less again.

The third season found my partner and me down in the same jungle chasing that same bull which we called *Mervin*. He played his game the same as the year before. He'd stay in the same spot, bugle and scream at us until we got too close, then he'd either shut up or just move ahead of us. We tried all kinds of strategies to get within bow range of that bull, only to be outsmarted time after time.

Several times while hunting, I'd listen for his bugles then just tried to sneak in on him. But because of the jungle of shin whackers he was in, that made it pretty much hopeless. One time Lester stayed up on the ridge and kept him bugling while I sneaked in on him. I knew I was in the area where I had last heard him, but he refused to bugle again. I decided to weasel through one more patch of alders, and was about halfway through, when not more than 30 yards in front of me the brush started shaking and crashing. Something big was coming toward me. I turned around and dove behind the closest tree, thinking the bull had heard me coming, thought it was another bull, and was charging. Everything was quiet for a while, then I caught a few glimpses of an elk through the brush and heard a loud screaming bugle. It was *Mervin*. He raked some brush, then crashed down the mountain and shut up for the rest of the day. Maybe I had only imagined that he had been coming at me, but he sure had me scared for a while. All I got accomplished that third season was playing cat and mouse games like that with *Mervin*. The end of the season came and he had me beat like usual.

On opening day of season four Lester and I were back in the same area and I was toting the same homemade bow and a quiver full of arrows. At the crack of dawn we spotted an elk across the drainage feeding in a clear-cut. He was too far away to make out any antlers, but once we saw him raise his head and then a faint bugle reached us. That was all it took for us to grab our bows and day packs and head his way at a good clip.

We guessed the elk was probably a small rag horn, the way he was out there in the clear-cut by himself. We were walking on an old logging road, figuring we were still a good ways from the bull. We decided to bugle to see if we could locate him. The last notes from Lester's bugle had just faded when the bull answered just around the bend in the road. I scrabbled for some cover beside the road while Lester streaked for a clump of dense trees a little farther back.

I had just gotten an arrow nocked and my head net over my face when I heard hoofbeats on the hard-packed dirt road. Then around the curve he came, and my eyeballs almost popped out of my head. This wasn't a small rag horn at all. I was looking at the biggest wild bull elk I had ever seen in my life. I watched him tip his nose up in the air, let out a deep bellow, and then topped it off with a row of chuckles. That bellow and the size of his rack gave him away right there. It was none other than *Mervin* himself, big as life, 30 yards in front of me and coming closer. My heart was doing double time and I felt myself losing my cool. I tried to force myself to pick a spot behind the shoulder and not look at the rack. There was only one tree between me and him, and as soon as he walked out the other side I'd smack him at 15 yards.

Would you believe it, that miserable bull stopped with the tree right over his vitals, turned his head, looked me right in the eye, and said, "Hah!" Well, I didn't hear it, but I know he said it. There I stood with my bow at half draw for a few seconds staring at the bull and the bull at me. Then he whirled and was gone, just like that.

That was the last we saw or heard old *Mervin*. I've hunted that area every September since, but never found any evidence he's still hanging out in that drainage. If he is, he's keeping well hidden and quiet when September rolls around and the other younger bulls squeal and challenge each other. Then again, he might be dead by now. Since he was a major bull already the first year we harassed him, he would be up in age by now. If he isn't amongst the living anymore, I hope he died a peaceful, natural death. A bull with his intelligence deserves nothing less.

We had our close encounter with *Mervin* on a Saturday. On Monday morning we were up on the same ridge again. Everything remained quiet until after the sun had hit the whole mountainside. Then we spotted a herd of elk about a mile out the ridge feeding in a clear-cut. We watched them for a while, until we counted four bulls in the herd.

With the warm weather we were having, and the bulls together in a herd like that, we thought the rut couldn't be going too strong yet. The best chance we had for those bulls, we decided, was to wait until we knew which way they would head to bed down for the day, then circle around and get in front of them. After waiting about an hour, they finally started up a narrow strip of timber between two clear-cuts. We grabbed our bows and packs and made tracks.

By the time we got to a little knoll overlooking the narrow strip of timber, we heard the elk uphill from us already. Since the timber was in a little draw and the sun wasn't hitting it yet, the thermal was downhill, with the elk moving against it. That had us stumped, because we hadn't accounted for that. The chance of calling a bull back downhill to where he'd just been seemed mighty slim, but it was the only card we had that was worth playing. So we made the best of it.

Our plan was to let Lester do the bugling and tree raking. If he didn't get an answer in 10 to 15 minutes he'd move ahead and do it over again, and so on until we'd bump into the elk or run them out of the country. I'd be the silent predator and just keep ahead of Lester 40 to 50 yards. Every time Lester would move ahead, I'd also sneak ahead. The first 20 to 30 minutes we didn't hear a single peep. So we moved farther and farther into the mass of alders and tules. Suddenly, about a stone's throw ahead I heard a racket that sounded like antlers raking a tree. Lester heard it too and got more aggressive. The noise ahead got louder. I moved ahead another 20 yards. Suddenly I heard the bull come crashing my way. The spot where I was standing wasn't an ideal place to shoot from at all, so I took a few more steps into a small opening where I could at least get the bow in front of me to draw.

By that time I saw the bull coming straight at me. He had his nose tipped up and his rack laid over his back. He had leaves and branches sticking in his brow tines and hanging over his face. The brush in front of him didn't faze him at all. He went right over it. There I stood with an arrow nocked, not knowing if he'd turn left or right, or maybe he wouldn't turn at all. The thought of getting run over flashed through my mind, but then ten yards in front of me the bull turned to my left. As he passed me at five yards, an arrow smacked into his rib cage and sliced through his heart. He kept right on going as if nothing had hit him for 20 yards. Beside Lester, the bull stopped. Not knowing if he was hit or not, Lester looked for a hole in the brush to thread an arrow through. Suddenly the bull's knees buckled and he hit the ground. I heard the crash and knew it was all over. I sat on a log to calm my nerves, and when I looked at the bow in my hand I noticed that it was trembling slightly, and my knees felt kinda weak too.

My thoughts went back three and a half years previously when I had glued together those first pieces of wood to build a bow to kill this first bull—how I had carried it with me over in Idaho. The bow had been with me when a mountain lion had stalked me one day in elk season. Another time when I was hunting alone a few miles from camp I had slipped and sprained my ankle. With the help of the bow as a cane I had limped to camp. Then for three seasons I had carried it with me in northwestern Montana while we chased old *Mervin*. I don't know how many times an arrow had been nocked. I had even started to draw on a bull a few times, but had never quite gotten a shot. Now, so suddenly, the bow, the bull, and I had connected.

Yep, I say to myself, it has been a long hunt …

did you know?

Only 230-300 Florida Key

whitetails remain in the wild.

Legendary Adventures

Whitetail Memories

DAVID YODER · *Millersburg, Ohio*

December 27, 2004 · Coshocton County, Ohio

MONDAY MORNING, OPENING day of muzzleloader season in 2004, didn't start off too well. Two of my brothers, one of our buddies, and I were planning on going deer hunting in Coshocton County. We got up in the morning, got ready, and waited, and waited, for our driver to show up. Due to a bad ice storm in the area three days earlier, he didn't show up. Needless to say, we weren't too happy. Luckily we found another driver and got to our hunting spot at 10:00, still having the rest of the day to hunt.

It was a beautiful morning with most of the ice from the storm still on the trees. It was 15°, and with the sun shining on the ice it was very beautiful. I sat on a tree stand at the back edge of a field in the middle of our property. Behind me the woods dropped down into a creek bottom. In front of me was a cornfield with the corn picked around the edges and still some standing in the middle.

At 11:30 three does came out and started feeding. I watched them for a while without getting a good shot. Finally they headed back towards the bedding area. One of them stopped at the edge of the field across from me at about 100 yards. I shot, and when the smoke cleared I saw it running into the woods. I reloaded and got down from the tree stand. One of the other guys came over and we went to see if we could find my deer. Sure enough, it had run about 100 yards and rolled over. We dragged it out and headed for the camper for a lunch break.

After lunch I headed back to the same tree stand again. It had warmed up to 23° by then. I didn't see much until about 4:00 some does and fawns started coming out to feed. A little later two little bucks came up and walked right under my tree stand. I was having a lot of fun watching all the does and little bucks when I looked down into the woods and saw two bucks. They messed around awhile, and the biggest buck in the field, an 8-pointer, went down and joined them. After awhile one of them started on up at an angle to pass about 80 yards from me. I recognized him right away and knew he was a shooter, as the other guys had seen him a couple of times that year. We had also watched him the year before. Since he had shot an 8-pointer earlier with the bow, one of the guys had passed him up on the last day of gun season from the stand where I was. The year before I had passed him up twice and the other guys also had a couple times, when he was much smaller. I had also found the one shed.

To get back to the story, the buck came up to about 80 yards and I saw I wouldn't get a better shot. So I shot, and he whirled and headed back down toward the creek. I saw him run for a couple hundred yards and thought I may have seen him limp a little bit. We waited until quitting time at 5:00, and then went and tracked a little bit. We found some blood and a piece of bone about an inch long. After tracking a couple hundred yards, we decided to wait until the next day to follow him.

My hopes weren't too high and I didn't feel the best that night. The next day we waited until noon, then my brother and I went on the trail. We tracked the deer down across the creek and up the other bank about 200 yards. All of a sudden he jumped up about 50 yards in front of us and stood behind some brush. I decided I could shoot through the brush. I shot and he turned and ran closer and stopped. With my gun empty, my brother asked, "Shall I shoot?"

I said, "Yes." So he shot and deer took off. We reloaded and followed. About 50 yards later we saw him standing about 30 yards away. I pulled up and shot, but he just stood there. We could see the blood pouring out where I hit him. My brother handed me his gun and I shot again, and the deer took off. We reloaded, followed the deer, and found him lying about 30 yards farther, almost done for. I finished him off with a shot in the neck. Out of six shots he had five holes in his body.

We estimated that the buck was about three and a half years old. He had ten points, with a 15½" spread. The longest tine was 11" and one G2 was forked. He grossed 140 inches—my biggest buck yet.

did you know?

The longest known horn length of a pronghorn antelope is 20 1/8" long.

Legendary Adventures

Black Powder in Colorado

MARVIN YODER · *Millersburg, Ohio*

"EURREEEEHU," THE FURIOUS bull screamed, and again came out to the edge of the meadow to look for this bull that was threatening to take his cows all morning.

It was 1:00 P.M. on September 8, 2004, when Jimmy, the packhorse, was finally loaded, and we boys, Ivan Miller, David Yoder, and I, shouldered our 20-pound frame packs and started our thirteen-mile hike. With some directions from the outfitter we were hoping to find our destination, a drop camp. On the way we saw a few grouse, muley does, and a cow moose.

Finally after six and a half hours of walking, we found the camp just before darkness settled in. It was a very welcome sight, with three tents waiting for us—one fair-sized cook tent, one gear tent, and one sleeping tent. To make things better yet, a bull chuckled 300 yards from camp ten minutes after we arrived. That helped us forget our tired bodies.

We had little to do the first night except unpacking, taking care of the horse, and then hitting the sack. We awoke at night to the sounds of an elk bugling and coyotes howling.

On Thursday morning, September 9, it was clear and a chilly 35°. We got up at 7:00. First we built a fire in the little stove and ate breakfast. Then we did some scouting and tried to find the basin where we were told to hunt. Unfortunately we were not able to find it the first day. We heard a bull bugle and saw a golden eagle. It was 4:30 when we returned to camp. We took care of the horse and ate supper.

In the evening I shot a few chipmunks with my slingshot. We took a little walk up the creek and heard a few bulls bugling. When we returned to camp we had a muley doe and fawn in our camp. We shot her twice with the slingshot before she stayed away.

It was cloudy on Friday morning, September 10, with a temperature of 45° and a light rain in the forenoon. We had pancakes and maple syrup for breakfast. Again we heard a bull chuckling and coyotes howling after daylight.

In the afternoon we saddled the horse and tied a rope to the pack saddle to help us get up the mountain. We set out again to find the basin. This time we found it, and everything was ready for opening day the next morning. In the evening the weather cleared and the elk started bugling again. We ate supper, dried some clothes, and went to bed.

Saturday, September 11, was opening morning. It was clear and 32°—a beautiful morning. We got up at 2:30, ate breakfast, and saddled Jimmy. By 3:45 we were on our way, taking turns leading the horse, with the other two holding on to the rope behind the horse. Our progress was not too bad. Finally, at our destination, David went to the upper end of the basin, Ivan in the middle, and I went to the bottom end.

David saw elk first. When he arrived at his spot he spooked a bull and a cow out of the basin. Later that morning, at 7:30, he shot a 4x4 at 50 yards. He made a good lung shot, but he had a little trouble finding the elk, since it rolled down a small cliff when it dropped.

Ivan was the next to score. While David and I were quartering David's bull, Ivan walked around the hillside to get Jimmy. All of a sudden he saw a bull standing in front of him at 70 yards. After a little sizing, he decided he wanted the elk, and dropped him with a backbone shot. It was a 4x5.

Later Ivan found another 4x5 rack on a dead carcass only a short distance away from his kill. By the time we got to skinning, the sun was hot and the flies were bad.

After we finished David's elk, David and Ivan took it out and started on Ivan's elk. I hiked higher up the mountain to find cell phone service. Finally climbing high enough, I called the outfitter to let him know we had two elk to pack out. I also called Doug, our carpenter driver at home, to let people in our area know how things were going.

Now we had the hard trip down the steep mountainside to camp with two elk and our hunting gear. David and Ivan each carried a quarter and their elk racks on frame packs, while I led poor Jimmy with approximately 300 pounds of meat on his pack saddle. We slowly made our way down the mountain. After an hour's hike of rough, downhill grade, and with some "good luck," we made it to camp safely.

With a few hours of daylight left to hunt, I went across the creek to a meadow nearby to sit until dark. I saw a few muley does and heard several bugles, but didn't see any elk or muley bucks. Later, after dark, we heard a bugle pretty close. After a warm supper of Ramen noodles, we were ready for a good night's rest.

It was partly cloudy on Sunday, September 12, another nice day at 55°. On that day we had an appointment at 12:00 noon to call the other members of our group, Doran Yoder, Robert Hershberger, and Abe Yoder. They were hunting about five GPS miles away in another camp. We hiked about four miles out the trail to find cell phone service. Talking with them, we had a few exciting stories to share. We had shot two elk and Robert had killed a nice 4x4 mule deer. The other two had passed on a few small bucks. Now with a full week of hunting left, we still had five buck tags, two bull tags, four black bear tags, and one archery elk tag. It looked like a long row to hoe, but we couldn't wait to do our best.

We each took a shower in the afternoon, as well as a nap. For supper we had fresh elk meat. That was a good treat. Again the elk were bugling in the distance.

Monday, September 13, was another nice, sunny day, but windy enough to be a little chilly. We got up at 3:00, ate breakfast, saddled Jimmy, and headed up the mountain. We reached our destination at 5:30. We left Jimmy behind, and after some good luck wishes we split up. David and Ivan went up higher to look for muley bucks while I went around the mountain to the basin. At daybreak I saw a few coyotes at David's kill site. I was very tempted to shoot, but feared I would spook elk close by.

An elk began bugling in the distance at 8:30, and was coming closer. I was soon bugling back. Finally they came closer and were heading to a pass 400 yards below me. I quickly worked my way downhill. All of a sudden I was too close, spooked a cow, and the whole herd ran back across the basin. But they stopped as soon as they got back to heavy timber. I started bugling and cow chirping again, and before long the bull elk was answering. This continued for about 45 minutes. A few times he would come out to the edge of the meadow to see who was challenging to take his cows.

Finally I quit calling and worked my way around to the bull's side of the meadow. Then I slowly stalked through the timber. All at once something caught my eye. A bedded cow was watching me at 40 yards, trying to figure me out. I stopped in my tracks, smiled to myself, and pulled up the bugle. This just had to work. One bugle is all it took. The bull answered right back and was on his way. I had my muzzleloader shouldered at 50 yards and was waiting for him to either stop or turn his side for a good shot. Instead he just kept coming closer, closer, closer. Finally, at 10 yards I was almost beyond control as I glanced across the barrel and pulled the trigger. "Kerboom!" As the smoke cleared away, the elk stood there, frozen in his tracks, trying to figure out what had happened. I put my gun down, poured the powder from the quickload, and was just ready to put the bullet down when the elk finally decided this was not for him. He took off around the mountain with his cows. That left me by myself wondering

140

what had happened. I had no idea if I had hit or missed.

After looking around, I found a few hairs and a little blood. Not finding much blood after half an hour, I slowly followed the tracks around the mountain. Luckily enough, after about 200 yards I spotted him bedded down and still alive. I rested down on one knee and shot again at 70 yards. He barely moved, so I walked up to him just in time to watch him expire. What a relief! The elk was a 32-inch wide 5x5.

Now came the butchering. First I rolled him on one side and skinned that down and took the quarters and backstraps off. Then I rolled him over and repeated the procedure. After about an hour's work, I had the quarters in the shade in garbage bags and the rack cut out. It was 12:00 noon.

I headed back to where we split up in the morning to get Jimmy. After staking Jimmy out in the meadow for some fresh grass, I took half an hour to get a little nap. Later I was just ready to saddle Jimmy when David and Ivan came off the mountain. It was good to see them, since I could use some help loading the meat.

After sharing some excitement, Ivan took the two frame packs and their guns and took the main trail to camp, while David and I went after my elk with Jimmy. David and Ivan had not found any muley bucks up on top, but they both had seen some elk, including two bulls.

We had a nice surprise when we returned to camp that evening. The outfitter was already there to pack out our meat. It did not take us long to decide to pack out with him and join the other camp for muley hunting. That evening we boned out the meat and packed a few things for the next morning. The meat was very good and cold yet. At night we would hang it in a tree. In the morning we took it down, rolled it in a tarp and threw old blankets and an old tent on top of it. That really worked great, with temperatures in the 20s at night and in the 60s in the daytime.

On Tuesday, September 14, it was nice and chilly again. We got up at 6:00 and ate breakfast. By 8:50 we had the four packhorses loaded and headed out the trail. Halfway out the trail we met some middle-aged guys from Missouri, packing in for a bow hunt. They were pretty tired, as they each had 50 or 60 pounds on their backs. It was 1:50 when we reached the trailhead. I suppose those rugged mountains at camp did us some good, since it took only five hours to pack out, and we were not nearly as tired.

After loading our gear on the truck and trailer, we headed for the second trailhead where the others were staying. Our outfitter had spent the night with us and came up short with chewing tobacco, so the first gas station was a must stop. We ate some ice cream and snacks, which was a good treat again. We stopped at the outfitter's home where we had our trailer parked with two freezers which we could plug in to keep our meat cold.

It was 6:00 that evening by the time we had Jimmy loaded again and were ready for the one-and-a-half-hour hike to camp. It was just dark when we arrived. They had told us there were plenty of muleys in the area, but were still surprised to see us so soon.

Abe had killed a buck that day. He found a group of bucks, and was trying to get closer for a shot, when he spooked them. So he followed them into the heavy timber, stalking slowly and carefully until he spotted one bedded behind a log, with only its head exposed. After a little hesitation, he aimed for the head and knocked the buck down. Not bad for a 60-yard shot, freehand, with an open-sighted muzzleloader. Ha! It was a nice 16-inch 4x4.

What an exciting evening in camp, with all six of us together. We had many stories to share. It was 10:30 when we finally headed for bed.

Wednesday, September 15, was another nice day. We all got up at 5:00 and ate breakfast, except Robert. We had a camp bug already. Ha! He only had a deer tag and filled it the first day. David went out with Doran on the rock ledge above camp, where they had spotted bucks the last few mornings. Abe went down below camp to look for elk or bears. Ivan went out the trail a ways and down in, while I went up to the top to some meadows.

It didn't take long to get some action going, as it was barely daylight when I spotted six bucks in a meadow. After some time with binocs, I picked out the biggest one and lay down to try the 100-yard shot. I was disappointed when only my cap went off. The deer all spooked and took off, except the biggest one. He thought he was going to check things out better before running. After putting another cap on, I quickly shot from behind yet, but missed. After reloading I hurried after them. A few meadows over I found them again. This time, sneaking up behind a tree, I laid my gun on a limb and tried again. After the smoke cleared, I watched the buck run about 50 yards, then go down. He was an 18-inch 3x3, still in velvet. After tagging my deer, I went back to camp to get Robert to help me quarter him.

In the meantime Doran and David had been doing a little shooting as well. They wounded two different bucks. So they helped me cut up mine, then we went back to look for the other deer. We soon found Doran's, as he had traveled only about 300 yards with a nasty gut shot. He was a 16-inch 3x4.

Later, while Robert, Doran, and I took our meat out to the freezer, David jumped the other wounded buck, which appeared to be hit in the front leg. He shot through some brush and missed him, and then had a nice open shot but his cap wouldn't fire. By the time he had the next cap on, the buck took off and he couldn't find him again.

In the evening David saw about 20 deer over in another canyon. There were only a few bucks, and nothing very close. Ivan saw two small bucks and two cow elk, but made no shots. Abe saw a few elk and called a spike bull in close, but it was not legal to shoot it. In the evening he saw two nice bucks, one about 24 inches, but poor Abe, he already had his buck.

The weather looked very nice again on Thursday, September 16. We got up at 5:00 and ate breakfast. Robert went out with Abe in the morning to look for elk. They went behind camp and out towards the road. Ivan and David went up to the top to some meadows to look for muleys. Doran still had an archery elk tag and I had a bear tag, so we hunted together. We headed east out of camp, back to a canyon where we usually got some elk action. We heard a few bugles and had a bull at 60 yards, but no shot.

On our way in we stopped by a neighboring camp and met Randy, Norman, and his wife. They were also deer hunting. Randy had just shot a good, heavy 24-inch 4x4 that morning.

David was the only one in camp at 11:30 when Robert and Abe came bursting into camp with an elk rack, and a lot of excitement. Robert had called the bull in and Abe had shot him through both lungs at 40 yards— a nice 6x6 with a 36-inch spread.

David saw ten bucks but passed on a few small ones. Ivan did not see much all day. Hopefully things will change for him.

On Friday, September 17, we got up at 5:00 and ate breakfast. Robert had some pancake mix along, but our breakfast was usually granola cereal with water and granola bars with some coffee or hot chocolate. In the daytime we would usually snack on trail mix and granola bars. For supper we had Ramen noodles, some Lipton meals, and fresh meat.

The weather looked beautiful again. Robert went with Doran in the morning, back to where we had seen some elk action the day before. David went up to the rock ledge above camp. Ivan went northwest below camp in the dark timber to look for muleys, while I went northeast below camp to look for bears. So far we had not seen a bear yet, so my chances looked pretty slim.

Robert and Doran had the best action of the day. Robert called a bull past Doran at 30 yards. The elk only offered good shots for Robert, but he wasn't hunting. Finally they got him stopped at 55 yards with a clear shot for Doran. He took the shot, and thought it looked okay from his viewpoint. Robert also saw the arrow and said the height looked good, but the penetration wasn't the best. Comparing information, they decided the shot was probably good.

After waiting for about an hour with pretty good hopes, they took up the blood trail. Unfortunately they didn't find what they expected, but only a shortage of blood and a very steep uphill incline. After a couple hundred yards they ran out of blood, and they gave up after looking around for another hour. The shot was possibly a little farther up front than they thought, and hit the shoulder, as the arrow was not in too far.

David had pretty good action too. In the morning he was stalking four bucks, including a nice 4x4. But they eluded him several times and disappeared into the timber before he got a shot. In the afternoon he found two bucks, a 3x3 and a 3x4. He finally worked his way to within 170 yards of the bigger one, and was waiting for a better angle yet, when the small one got his wind and they took off. Again, so close but still so far away.

Bear hunting was the same. We still did not find any.

Ivan's luck had not changed much yet. He just saw a few does in the afternoon.

It was the last night at the campfire, so we sat out a little later, until about 11:00.

It was a little cloudy the morning of Saturday, September 18. We planned to hunt until noon, and then pack up camp and head out. Doran went back to look for his elk again. He didn't find any more signs, but stumbled on a muley buck at 15 yards.

Ivan went up to the top to hunt the meadows. His luck finally changed as he shot a 3x3 by 9:00. He dropped it with a backbone shot at 165 yards. What a great shot on the last-minute buck.

I went with David up on the rock ledge to try his luck on a buck yet. At first all we saw was a forky, and he spotted us and ran off. Well, it was crunch time, so we took off, trying to cover as much area as possible. About half an hour later we spotted a herd of six, coming off the far top. They were far enough away that we couldn't see any racks with the binocs, but we were pretty sure they were bucks.

Well, it was a long ways back there, but it looked like that might be our only hope, so off we went. Every time we topped a knoll, we stopped and glassed to watch if they would come down on our side, or if they went down the back side. Finally we got back to the last knoll and stopped and paused. We couldn't see anything, so we took off for our last gully.

Whoa! Whoa! There they were, 150 yards away on the other side, and they had already seen us. We were caught in the middle of nowhere, with no good rest for the gun, and they were heading out. Finally they stopped at 280 yards, and David took a desperation shot but came up empty. The two best bucks of the group were a velvet 3x3 that had to be about 30 inches wide and a 4x4 close to 24 inches. So much for one last try, leaving the two of us shaking our heads.

On the way back to camp we did get another chance at a forky at 167 yards steep uphill. David missed him twice. He was probably shooting over his back.

We were not far from camp when I realized that I had lost Robert's range finder. What buck fever can't do! I thought I remembered where we might have lost it, all the way back where we had shot at the bucks. David went in to start packing up camp, and I went after the range finder. The only good thing was that I found it exactly where I had lost it.

It was 2:00 by the time we were ready to start out. With two packhorses to help, the journey was not too bad. We took most of David's gear so he could hunt on his way out yet. He saw one elk and one deer, but did not shoot.

We went home with five bucks and four bulls. The tags we had left were one muzzleloader mule deer, one bow elk, and four muzzleloader bears.

Good fellowship, a good driver, and good hunting contributed to a wonderful trip.

Courtesy of Jonas Mast.

Cozy elk camp in Colorado.

Courtesy of Jonas Mast.

Packing out elk in a Colorado snowstorm.

Rapid mountain stream in Colorado.

Awesome rugged country in Wyoming.

Nice Wyoming mule deer.

Arizona gray fox with bow.

Arizona javelina.

Awesome view of the Colorado Rockies.

Falls in Quebec, Canada.

Hunting and trapping tepee.

Courtesy of Ervin Yoder.

Courtesy of Jonas Mast.

Deer Story—2003 (pg. 17).

Packing in high country Colorado.

Courtesy of Ura Allen Erb.

Second-chance buck (pg. 69).

My 6-point bruiser.

6 x 6 Elk, Colorado.

Where Dan Mast shot his bear (pg. 47).

Our cozy cabin on a Quebec
bear hunt (pg. 61).

Packing out muleys in Wyoming.

Sundown in Wyoming.

An excellent Idaho elk hunt.

A mule deer hunt in Utah. *Courtesy of Dan Mast.*

Arizona desert bighorn sheep. *Courtesy of Dan Mast.*

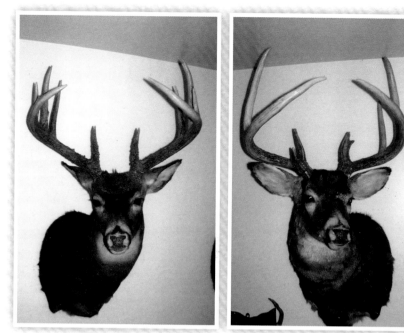

Courtesy of Dennis Raber.

The last-minute buck.

Courtesy of Dennis Raber.

Another nice 8-pointer.

Courtesy of Crist Nisley.

Awesome cactus country in Arizona.

Courtesy of Jonas Mast.

Bear camp in Quebec.

Gorgeous sunset in Arizona.

The jumping cactus in Arizona—
barbs are drawn by static—very painful.

Joe Erb's sheep with guide in British Columbia in 1964.

Taking a break with our packhorses in British Columbia in 1964.

Cozy camp in British Columbia glassing for grizzlies in 1964.

The rugged terrain in British Columbia where we hunted in 1964.

Joe Erb's trophy collection of British Columbia in 1964.

Ed Kline's sheep taken in British Columbia in 1964.

Eli J. Yoder's grizzly bear taken   150 Class Kentucky buck (pg. 43).
in British Columbia in 1964.

Elk hunting in the Rockies (pg. 25).

Poor Jimmy was very overloaded on opening day, coming
back to camp, but he did a great job.

Tuesday morning, just out of camp, heading for the trailhead.

Challenging the rugged but awesome country.

Courtesy of Chris Leply.

Chris Leply and his trophy buck (pg. 91).

Courtesy of Ed Yoder

Ed Yoder with his kudo bull from Africa.

The Bob Marshall Blues

BEN MILLER · *Rexford, Montana*

THE BOB MARSHALL Wilderness area is located in north-western Montana, directly below Glacier National Park. It is at least 100 miles long and approximately 40 miles wide. The wilderness area has no roads and allows no motorized vehicles, or any motor for that matter, within the wilderness boundaries. Horses and mules are the only means of transportation in this place, other than on foot. No logging is done in the wilderness, although around it is lots of national forest open to timber harvesting.

Of course, the Bob Marshall harbors much game and many outfitters guide hunters to trophy elk and mule deer within its perimeter.

I have personally been in the Bob Marshall twice and each time I was awed by the broad valleys and tall, jagged peaks hoisting their snow-capped spires up into the clouds. The first time I was in this area was with my cousin and three other guys in July of '06. We were on an exploring trip just for pleasure. The only deadline we had was to be out at a certain trailhead to be picked up on a Saturday. We had enough horses for four of us, but the fifth had to walk and lead one of our two pack animals. Two of us shared a packhorse and the three others shared a mule. Anyhow, we had an all-out blast. We rode probably 55 miles on our trip. We moved camp every day and used a different rock for a pillow every night.

The second time I was in the Bob was during the September early rifle season. This time we meant strict business. No moving camp every day, and no unnecessary sight-seeing. Nope, all jokes aside, we were huntin' elk and muleys. My first cousin, Junior, was the "guide" on this trip. He'd been to the area we'd planned to hunt a few times before, but hadn't been there for around fifteen years.

After much map stabbing and planning we got our act together. We had hopes of having nice weather, but we were prepared for the worst. Tents, tarps, ropes, twine, matches, compasses, rain gear, rubber boots, and, yes, we even included a roll of toilet paper, a necessary luxury even for a wilderness experience.

On this trip we each had a pack animal and we loaded 'em good. My packhorse was a tough-hided critter whose front feet turned out like those of Daffy Duck. At times he'd kick those duck feet against grass clumps and stumble, but he was a decent pack animal anyway.

On the way in we heard a bull bugling down in a steep drainage, which got the blood fired up. We arrived around 4:00 P.M. and immediately set about staking our horses or tying them to highlines, and also to setting up some tarps and the tent.

By the time we were all set up and firewood was cut, it was dark. So we checked guns, packed day packs, and prepared gear for an early start in the morning. Junior slept in his tent and I slept under the tarp by the fire.

Tuesday morning dawned with a grin and we dished up a breakfast that'd make the White House chef throw in the towel. The only thing that gent of the cookin' utensils wouldn't have put up with was the pieces of white ashes on the grub.

We lost a little time that morning because Junior didn't know exactly where we were. But along about daylight he spotted a ridge where he said they used to sit to glass for elk, so we made tracks for that spot. A half hour later we eased over the top of the ridge and got settled comfortably in a huckleberry bush to glass the other side.

Well, we looked through 'em magnifying tubes for a while, then dug out snacks from our day packs and conversed in low tones. Nothing was stirring and I was getting a little antsy to look over some more ridges, so I bid my partner *adios* and sneaked off downhill.

I crossed the bottom and started climbing up the other side, which was steep for a couple yards, leveled off on a bench, then was steep again with another bench, and so on until close to the top. I spent quite a bit of time on that first bench, though, as there were huckleberries hanging thickly all over the bushes. I ate until my mouth was purple, then kept on climbing. At almost every heavy-laden berry bush I'd stop and strip it, and then keep going.

I finally reached the top and poked my eyebrows over the top to see what was on the other side. Another beautiful drainage lay down below, and I scored it well with my binoculars, but saw no horned critters. Finally I rose and moved off to my left, staying just below the top of the ridgeline so as not to be silhouetted against the skyline.

I walked along for perhaps a half mile and was seeing quite a bit of sign of muleys, so I kept my eyes peeled. The ridge rose sharply and formed into a peak, and I figured this would be a dandy place to sit and glass. Sure enough, when I got to the top I could see that the other side opened up into an awesome sloped valley, leading down almost to the river.

I sat on top and glassed down, but wasn't quite satisfied, for I could see only part of the slope. I decided to move down into the saddle where I could get a better view. That valley sure struck me as one that should have game in it. I went down sort of behind the peak and stayed down in the trees, then circled around and came up in the saddle.

I no more than stepped out and looked down, when I saw at least four muley bucks bounding downhill. I could see at least a few were nice bucks. I couldn't shoot from where I was, so I quickly moved a little farther left and down a bit. I squatted on my haunches and pointed the business end of my bean shooter downhill. Thinking I was running out of time, I hurriedly found one of the nicer bucks in my scope, aimed a little low to compensate for steep ground, and touched off.

Fire belched from the muzzle and the hillsides played kickball with the echo until they lost it downhill. I could see that it was a clean miss, so I quickly jacked another shell in and held just above the hindquarter. The gun was hardly done kickin' when all of a sudden the buck lost control and went rolling down the hill, head over heels, horns over hindquarters. He didn't roll far until he was outa sight, but I could still hear a commotion goin' on down below.

Now I had time to look around and, lo and behold, there stood probably the biggest buck I'd ever seen in the wild, a little farther down the hill from where I'd shot mine. That old boy would run about 40 yards, then stop and shake his head, then run a short distance and do it again. By that time I was wishing like all git out that I'd spent more time trying to locate the biggest one in the herd.

Finally I decided that maybe the one I shot wasn't so small after all, and I got up and started slippin' and slidin' down the slope. Rounding a knob in the hillside I saw the buck I shot down below, still trying to get up. Quickly charging down to him, I ended his misery with one shot to his neck. And boy, did that buck ever look small compared to that big ol' boy I'd just watched jog off.

Well, now here's where the work began. I stripped to the waist and started guttin' the deer. I then skinned and quartered him on the spot. All the time I was working I was eyeballing that steep slope I'd have to pack him up, and the smaller rack on that buck sure wasn't helping matters any either.

To make a long story short, after I'd made two trips down there and back up on top I just lay there, all stretched out on the ground, for maybe fifteen minutes, resting so I could get back to camp. All the way back to camp I kept trying to convince myself that my antlers weren't really that bad. He had a 20-inch outside spread and was a 3x4, but not very heavy. I finally had to console myself with the idea of coming back next year and pluggin' that big one.

Back at camp Junior kept passing remarks about my little buck and so on, but I came back at him by asking him to show me *his* rack. Of course he hadn't gotten anything yet.

That night it turned cold, and man, did it ever snow. In the morning there were ten inches of white stuff on the ground. Junior and I huddled around our smoky campfire trying to make breakfast. Junior told me that he woke up in the middle of the night and the snow load on his tent had squashed the top down to within a couple of inches of his face. He'd just taken his fist and bashed it back up.

We had planned to get the rest of my mule deer quarters that day and hunt on the way there and back, but the visibility was down to a couple yards. The bear grass slopes were slippery and we had to scratch for footing. Glassing for game was out of the question, as it was way too cloudy. We got the meat and went back to camp.

That night it got cold and the horses shivered and shook until finally Junior and I decided to saddle them up for the night. The rest of the week up there was a dreary, rainy drag. We'd try to hunt, but would come back cold and soaked to the skin.

Finally, we decided to pack out a day early. Back down at the trailhead the sky had cleared off somewhat. We built ourselves a fire and cooked some grub, then stowed our saddles and gear in the horse trailer so we'd be ready to go when our driver came to haul us home.

If any of you readers ever attempt a wilderness adventure like this, my advice is to expect the best but prepare for the worst. In my opinion a few 12' x 14' tarps are better than small tents and are much lighter than a wall tent. Some neat, cozy shelters can be built out of them. Rain gear is a must. Woolen pants are a very wise and comfortable choice. Woolen clothing is warm even when wet. Of course, good footgear is a moot point. I wore the Muck Boot brand boot for wet conditions, although they lacked in traction on those steep slopes. My leather hunting boots are Cabela's Meindle brand with 400 grams insulation. Another word of caution. Don't depend on Gore-Tex shoes to keep your feet dry in extremely wet conditions.

I'm already looking forward to another pleasure trip down to the Bob Marshall this summer. Of course, we'll take the packhorses and probably stay for a week. If any of you readers have a hankering to see this place, I advise you to pack up and go! Just remember, many are called but few are chosen.

did you know?

The largest moose antlers recorded have a

spread of 78 1/2", with 43 prongs.

Joe's Twelve-Pointer

JOSEPH P. YODER (AGE 13) · *Millersburg, Ohio*

2005 · Coshocton County, Ohio

IT WAS MONDAY morning, the first day of gun season. I was in eighth grade and was supposed to be in school, but our freezer was running low on meat so I decided I would rather go hunting instead. Dad, my brother Reuben, and I went to our hunting grounds. It was a very rainy morning. Dad and I were on a two-man tree stand. It was about 10:45 A.M. We hadn't seen any deer all morning.

About that time we saw a little flick of white moving on the other side of a creek bottom behind a briar patch, about 100 yards away. We kept watching and looking with binoculars, when finally after about 15 minutes we saw antlers moving. The deer was still too far away with too much brush to shoot from the stand. So we unloaded our guns, let them down, and started to sneak after the buck we had seen.

Then it began to drizzle again, just enough to cover our sound. We came to within 60 yards, but couldn't get through the briars. We decided I would just try my luck from where I was. Dad put his gun down on the ground. He had shot a little three-pointer during the bow season. He thought it was a doe until after he shot. The antlers were so small he didn't see them until he was up close. But it was too late! As a result he couldn't shoot at another buck this season.

After Dad put his gun down and covered his ears with his hands, he told me to use his shoulder for a rest for my gun. I aimed, pulled the trigger, and shot at the deer. It ran up a little hill on the other side of the creek. We made our way through the briar patch for about 10 yards and stopped for another shot. This time the deer stumbled and almost fell, but he kept on going until he was out of sight. We crossed the creek bottom and started up the hill after it. We didn't go far until we found the deer lying in a ravine.

My heart throbbed with excitement when I saw what I really shot. It was a heavy 12-pointer that officially scored 158-7/8.

This was the first deer I shot. Not too bad for a start—much more fun than a day in school.

The Baler Twine Hunt

ATLEE YODER · *Rexford, Montana*

AFTER APPLYING FOR a bighorn sheep ram tag for a number of years, and not having any success, I realized the odds of drawing a ram tag anywhere in the lower 48 states is pretty slim. When a friend of mine drew a ewe tag in a special unit several hundred miles south of my home in western Montana, and told me of the numbers of sheep in that area, I decided to apply for a ewe tag also.

I had decided if I got the tag I'd sure try and get the sheep with the longbow. I've always been a longbow freak when it comes to hunting. Some of my friends think I'm silly, but that doesn't bother me in the least because I'd say all hunters are silly one way or another. Well, I got the tag the first year I applied.

So the last week in October four buddies and I were hiking along the Clark Fork River, leading four horses loaded with camping supplies and enough grub to last us for a week. This was new territory for all five of us. I'd be concentrating totally on bighorn sheep for the hunt. Dennis, Jerry, and Daniel came along to see if they could rake together some elk or muleys to harass. Even a black bear wouldn't be safe in these hills, as we had a couple tags in our pockets. The fifth fellow, Bert, was along just kinda for the experience. He had just recently moved to the West from Indiana, so he wasn't carrying any hunting license or tags.

We finally found the stream we had picked out on the map to follow upstream until we found a camping spot to our liking. We were making our way up a steep, open slope along the creek when I noticed that the load on my horse was slipping. I quickly laid my bow on the ground and walked back to shift the load. Well, I kinda got Shorty off balance and he took a few steps and stepped right smack-dab between my bow limb and the string. Dennis was coming up behind me and, seeing the predicament I was in, dropped his lead rope and came to my aid. While we were concentrating on getting the bow out from around Shorty's leg, the pack suddenly slipped down under his belly. He sure didn't fancy having some bundles hanging down amongst his legs, and showed that by bucking and kicking, with my bow waving around in the air until the string broke.

Eventually Shorty got himself in a position where his backbone was hugging mother earth and his legs were pointing at the clouds. We quickly opened the snaps and the latigo and relieved him of the load. We got the horse back on his feet again and picked up some scattered items. Nothing was damaged much except the bowstring. I felt like kicking myself for not putting an extra string in my pack. All through archery season I had that on my mind—I needed to get an extra string made to put in my day pack—but I kept forgetting until I was out in the woods again. Now I had forgotten one time too often and this happened. Oh well, if nothing else, I'd just have to do all my sheep hunting with the rifle. I had brought it along too, just in case the sheep hunting was tougher than I thought. I had already decided time and money wouldn't allow me to make a second trip.

Finally we got Shorty reloaded again, but left behind about a third of the load. Somebody would have to come back and pick it up later, as we had been pushing the weight limits on this load from the beginning. We were getting close to where we wanted to set up camp and had fanned out, looking for the best spot. Suddenly Dennis let out a yelp and said he had been stung. A yellow jacket, for no reason at all except that he may just have had a craving to sting something at that minute, had stung him in the arm. Now for any of us other guys, getting stung wasn't such a big deal, but it so happens that Dennis is allergic to bee stings and had previously had some serious reactions from a sting. He didn't have his needle along to give himself a shot but did have some pills in his day pack. Yet we weren't sure which load held his pack. By the time we found his pack we had three horses unloaded.

We decided, since we had everything unloaded and scattered, this would be the best spot to set up camp. Bert unloaded his horse and, taking another saddle horse, he went back down the trail to fetch the rest of Shorty's dumped load. Luckily Dennis had no reaction from the yellow jacket sting, and he and I were occupied with setting up the wall tent. Daniel began stringing up highlines and taking care of the stock. Jerry dug out an apple, sat on a stump, and began eating. In between bites he gave plenty of advice how this and that should be done. We had to remind him a couple times that the only reason we asked him to come along on this hunt was because we needed his horse and wall tent.

We finally had everything set up. Bert had returned with the dropped load and had taken care of the stock. The water jugs were all filled, the tent stove was throwing heat, and Jerry was finished sucking on his apple core. The sun was still up, promising us another hour of daylight. So everybody hiked out a short distance from camp on some high points to look for game and to see what the country around us looked like.

After dark, when we all gathered at camp, every one of us had seen muleys, and Jerry also had spotted a bear and some elk, but no bulls. After we had fed our faces that night I took some baler twine and patched my bowstring the best I could. After shooting a few arrows I decided it would do, although the bow didn't shoot quite the same and had some more hand shock.

On Tuesday morning Bert and I saddled our horses and headed up a trail that led to the top of the mountain we were on. I planned to turn the horses over to Bert once we had gained enough elevation and make a big circle down toward the river on foot. Bert would take my horse back to camp.

Only about 30 minutes after I left Bert and the horses on the trail, I came over a small finger ridge and spotted a black bear across a deep ravine on the opposite side. Well, I had a bear tag in my pocket, and the bear was right where I was headed anyway, so I thought I might as well give him some trouble. After I picked out a lone tree with the top broken off and a big light green bush as landmarks close to the bear, I headed down into the deep ravine and then up the other side.

Once I came within a couple hundred yards of my quarry, I slowed down and tried picking my way through the loose shale scattered all over the slope. One step at a time, I slowly inched forward, sometimes using my limb tip as a third foot. But it was impossible to keep from making any noise. It seemed like all I had to do was just look at a piece of shale and it would go rattling down the slope.

Finally I knew I had to be past the spot where the bear had been. It didn't surprise me at all when I didn't find the bear. Coming through that shale slope was plenty to give myself away. Although I hadn't noticed the broken tree or the light green bush, I assumed things just didn't look the same from the different angle. Oh well, just a bear. After all, I had a more important tag in my pocket to notch. I quickened my pace and had gone 50 to 75 yards farther, when suddenly I noticed a broken tree and a light green bush. Just like that, I came around a bush and there was the bear.

Bears naturally don't have good eyesight and mostly depend on their noses. Since I had the wind on this fellow, I had him stumped. He stood there broadside at 30 yards trying to figure me out and gave me plenty of time to nock an arrow and draw down on him. I saw my fletching disappear right behind his shoulder and then heard it bouncing over rocks behind the bear. The bear never seemed to notice anything happened to him and slowly turned and climbed up on a huge log behind him. I loosed another arrow while he was on top of the log and got him right in the heart. I nocked the third arrow as the bear dropped off the log on the other side.

Everything was quiet for awhile, then I heard a few whines and moans from behind the log. The bear had been uphill from me and suddenly came rolling out from behind the log and went rolling down the slope in front of me. I saw the ghost had left him, and after he rolled out of my sight I still heard brush popping and shale rattling down below. When everything quieted down, I scooted down the slope after the bear and found him lodged in behind a tree. Seeing this was not the type of spot to skin a bear, I shoved him down the slope again and then followed. I had to do this a few times until I had him in the bottom of the ravine.

After I had skinned and deboned the bear I followed my backtrail to where I had left Bert and the horses. Bert had tied my horse, Shotgun, to a tree along the trail that morning and said he was gonna ride to the look-out tower all the way on the top, and then pick up Shotgun on the way down. Since only a couple hours had passed since we parted, I expected to beat Bert to my horse. Sure enough, Shotgun was still by the trail. After hanging my jacket on a low branch so Bert would recognize that I had taken Shotgun, I climbed into the saddle and headed for camp.

I had just put the packsaddle on Shorty and was hunting my cargo ropes when Bert rode into camp. After I filled him in on my story, he was itchin' to go along and pack out the bear. We rode our saddle horses as far as we could until we got to where we had to side hill over some loose shale, then we tied the saddle horses to trees and led Shorty from there.

Getting the horse to the bear in the ravine wasn't at all a walk in the park, but we got in and out without any mishaps. By the time we had the bear meat on the meat pole it was dark and the other hunters started filing in. Everyone had seen mule deer again, but no big bucks. Jerry had seen the same cinnamon-colored bear that he had seen the evening before, but he had filled his bear tag earlier in the season. Daniel had spotted a big-horn sheep ram bedded down on a sunny slope.

On Wednesday morning Bert and I did the same thing again. I hunted downhill on foot and he brought my horse back to camp. This time no bear got in my way and I got a little farther from camp. By midday I was perched high on a ledge eating some snacks and soaking up the sunshine. I hadn't found any sheep at all. I thought I was probably hunting too high in the timber, and as soon as I finished my snack I'd drop down lower among the cliffs and ledges.

Suddenly I heard a faint tick. I thought it came from my bow, so I picked it up, inspected it, and laid it down again. A few minutes later I heard the same sound. I inspected the bow again, couldn't see anything wrong with it, and laid it back down. A few minutes later I heard it again. This time I knew it was the bow. I just got my hand on the bow when it went, *ping*. Pieces of string flew out over the ledge. After I had fixed the string with baler twine the first evening and tested it I had only made two shots and those were the two bear shots. Had I wanted to take a shot at a sheep that morning the bow would probably have blown up. I dug into my day pack for some more baler twine and soon had my bow fixed up with a brand-new string again.

That afternoon I did get into sheep—three ewes and a half curl ram. I got pretty close but was on a ledge about 40 feet above 'em. I watched 'em for awhile and tried to figure out how to get down to their elevation. After a bit I noticed the sheep were climbing up toward my ledge. Quickly I inspected my ledge. It was about 15 yards wide and in the middle was a pickup-sized rock. The sheep would have to come around one side or the other of that rock.

I picked the right side and pulled my head net over my face and huddled up against a rock. In a few minutes they came, two ewes, with the half curl ram bringing up the rear. The other ewe was still down over the edge somewhere. The three came right at me until they got to the end of the rock ledge. Instead of coming around my side they chose the other. As soon as the ram had disappeared behind the rock, I pussy-footed over to the rock thinking maybe I could ease around the side and get a close-up quartering-away shot at the lead ewe. As I poked my head around the rock the ewe happened to be coming around the other side, facing me. We saw each other at the same time at a distance of about ten feet. I'm pretty sure I saw her eyes bug out, but what amazed me was how quietly those sheep left that ledge. There was just a flash and I was alone. I'm not even sure what happened to them. All I can figure out is that they whirled behind the rock and jumped over the edge of the 40-foot cliff.

I sneaked over to the edge and took a peek in the direction of the ewe that had stayed behind. Sure enough, she was still there, not even having noticed that her partners had spooked. After a while I knew she'd be coming up the same path the others had. This time I backed up a little farther against a tree. I decided I'd rather take a 20-yard shot than a 5-yard quartering toward me.

After a few minutes the ewe came. At 20 yards I let 'er fly. The arrow hit with a loud whack, and I got that sickening feeling that probably every bow hunter has experienced one time or another. As she jumped over the ledge I saw that all the penetration I had gotten was only a little more than the broadhead.

I couldn't imagine what went wrong. Everything felt good when I released. It was just as if the arrow had strayed off about four inches and lodged right in the shoulder. I searched around the cliffs and ledges for a while but never found a drop of blood.

When I got to camp that night a bunch of sheds hung on the ridgepole that the other hunters had brought in. The main story was that Dennis had gotten a hankering to have a cinnamon-colored bear hide, and had wandered off in the direction Jerry had seen that one twice. He had connected and came back to camp for horses. Bert was there at the time, so they each took a saddle horse, and Shorty for a packhorse, and brought the bear back. On the way to camp Shotgun got Shorty's lead rope under his tail while going through a rock slide and began running and bucking. Dennis said he took one glance at all the rocks going past down below and made up his mind to stay with the leather.

On Thursday Bert decided to tag along with me for the day. We rode our horses out of camp for a mile or so. Then we unsaddled and hunted on foot. We spotted several different herds of sheep that day, but got closer to killing ourselves than any sheep. I got to about 40 yards from the first group, which is still out of my range, then they became suspicious and moved off. The next group was high up in some cliffs and we actually got within bow range, but I hadn't been expecting sheep when they showed up and they had me pinned without my bow in hand. We got into some hair-raising spots up there. At several places one slip would have meant certain death. We kinda learned that some of that country wasn't designed for the human race. It was a relief in the evening when we got both feet on level ground again.

That night we added some more sheds to the collection on the ridgepole. Nobody had yet seen a bull elk or a shooter muley buck, although there seemed to be plenty of cows and does in the area.

Friday morning Dennis and Bert tagged along, looking for sheep. We were scheduled to be picked up Saturday at noon and thought we would take all morning to pack up camp and head out. So if I wanted to notch my sheep tag, I'd have to do it today.

I shouldered my longbow in the morning and stuck my rifle in the scabbard in case it would come to that. Then the three of us rode out of camp. It didn't take us long to spot a sizable bunch high above us. I was afraid if I blew this stalk we might not be able to find any other sheep all day. Bert said he'd come along and carry my rifle for me until I got to the final stalk, then I could switch weapons if I wished. Dennis stayed down by the river to watch the show through his binoculars. Bert and I started climbing rocks. We had only a couple hundred yards between us and the sheep, but noticed that we would have to cross some of that loud shale again.

We decided Bert would wait there and I would sling the rifle over my shoulder until I got within sight of the sheep. I was slowly picking my way through the shale, knowing the sheep were just ahead over a little rocky knoll. I happened to look up at the right time to see an adult ewe jump up on a rock in plain sight about 75 yards up ahead. She spotted me right away, and I knew that in a few seconds she would jump out of my sight again and might spook the whole herd on the other side of the knoll. If she did, this might be my last chance. I quickly dropped the bow, whipped the rifle off my shoulder, took aim, and squeezed off. She took one jump and was out of sight, but from where Bert sat he saw her collapse. I hurried up to the top of the knoll and saw her lying there. I waved my orange vest as a signal for Dennis to head on up to help with the skinning and packing.

Well, I got my sheep tag notched, which is more than a lot of people get to experience, and I should have been satisfied. But it still bothered me that I had gotten a nice bow shot at a ewe and had just wounded her. Maybe the stupid baler twine had something to do with it; maybe not. It had worked fine for the bear, but at that time I had the real string except for six inches of baler twine. For the sheep I had an all-twine string. I would probably have made a bad shot anyway, but still if I would have stuck an extra string in the pack before I left home, I could have saved a lot of foolishness.

However, what really got my dander up was when I wanted to empty my day pack to fill it with sheep meat. I turned the day pack upside down, shook it, and out of an inside pocket fell a spankin' new bowstring, which I had been carrying with me all season without knowing it!

List of fatal bear attacks in North America

1910-1919...... 1

1940s.............. 1

1960s.............. 2

1970s.............. 3

1980s.............. 8

1990s.............. 8

2000s............ 19

The Joy of Taking the Next Generation Hunting

ELI WENGERD · *Dundee, Ohio*

AS WE ENJOY the wild outdoors, whether it is for a walk, or to do some hunting or scouting, do we remember to take our younger generation along to teach them the ways of the great outdoors? This can be in a lot of different ways.

When our girls were younger we built a cabin in the woods to use for hunting and as a family retreat. We spent many days on the project. One of the girls was on a scaffolding and put barn siding on the 16-foot-high peak of the ceiling. I will always remember her saying with a grin on her face, "If Mom would see me now." Also, one day we cut the 8x8 mantle piece to length and two small girls and Dad looked at it and said, "Sure, we can get it up on there." Then sitting back and smiling at what we had accomplished.

We as a family also have many great memories of the girls going along deer hunting. It was always such a great feeling when they got a deer, especially their first one. Sometimes they think they are better hunters than Dad. One year one of the girls didn't go too much in the first part of the bow season. I think the reason for this was she had another type of dear on her mind, and yes, she did get that one too!

Finally, on the first Friday evening in November, she said, "Dad, I want to go along hunting."

We prepared ourselves and she sat at her favorite spot on the ground in the brush. After putting more brush around her, I went for my stand. About half an hour before dusk she called me on the walkie-talkie and said, "I hit one and it ran into the brush."

I told her to go to the cabin and I would be there at dark. Well, we went to look and she had a doe shot through the heart and it had run only 20 yards. What a proud hunter, as Dad did not even have to do the gutting.

The next Friday evening she said, "Dad, I want to go along again."

I asked her, "Where do you want to sit?"

She smiled and said, "That one spot is always pretty good."

So we got her settled in and I went for my stand again. I didn't hear from her, so I went to the cabin at dark where I found her with a big smile. She said, "Are you ready to go look for him?"

Off we went to look for what she said was a buck. We found the blood trail and followed it for about 50 yards and there was a six-point buck, shot through both lungs.

Well, about now I was wondering if I smelled bad or what was wrong with me. Yet it was more fun to see her get those two deer than getting one myself. I tried to tell everyone that I taught them so well; it was just like an old Indian passing his wisdom on to the younger generation, but no one would buy that. Everyone said they thought the girls were just better hunters than I was.

As we journey through life, let us remember to teach our younger ones the ways of the great outdoors, in hunting, fishing, birding, or nature hiking, because all too soon they will be on their own, and then we will need to start thinking about taking the grandchildren along.

The Turkey Story

ELI WENGERD · *Dundee, Ohio*

AS WE GO wandering about in the great outdoors, I'm sure we all have some of the most unique things happen to us. Sometimes we win and sometimes the creatures win by outsmarting us. Here's a true story about a turkey that outsmarted me and left with a grin on his face and turkey *doo-doo* on mine.

Prior to the season opening, I had gone to the edge of a woods to listen for turkeys, to see where they were roosting. By listening a couple mornings, I thought now the real turkey hunter had them figured out.

Opening morning found me on a knoll uphill from where they should be roosting, with a nice view of the area to make sure they didn't slip by unseen. As daylight came, the gobbling started below me in the hollow. As time went on, I saw them fly off the roost, but they went to the side and up the hollow. By then there was a frustrated turkey hunter who had been outsmarted.

Not to be outdone by these creatures, I told myself the next morning I would move in closer on them. I picked out two trees and very early the next morning I was on my little seat nestled between the trees. Now I knew I would be right in the roosting area, so I could not move or they might see me. The early light of dawn was peeping through and there still were no gobbles. More daylight, and still there was nothing. Yet I was careful not to move, since they could be close.

Legendary Adventures

At one point I thought I heard something drip into the leaves but figured it was water from the trees. My hearing is not good in the woods. I heard it again, only this time I smelled something that brought back memories of cleaning out the chicken coop on the farm.

I told myself, wouldn't it be very funny if there was a turkey above me in the tree. I looked up very slowly, and way up high above me was a turkey in the tree. There was not much to do except hold still so he would not see me. I kept watching him as he scratched his head and stretched his wings, totally unaware of my presence right below him. Finally he turned around on the limb, so I thought he must be about ready for takeoff. All of a sudden, like an old man with chewing tobacco, he sent a big load my way. Some of it landed around me on the ground and a drop went on my box call next to me. After feeling he had his mission accomplished, the turkey flew, way up into the woods, and I never did get a shot at him.

I took a pen and circled the spot on my box call so we would never forget it. When I came home and was telling my wife about this historic event, she asked, "What is that spot below your eye?"

I went and looked in the mirror and, sure enough, it was a spot of turkey *doo-doo*.

Needless to say, I had enough humor that morning so I did not need to shoot a turkey. Looking back on the whole episode, I am just sure I saw a smirk on the turkey's face as he flew up through the woods.

Bear Hunting Story

WAYNE MAST · *Fryburg, Ohio*

IT IS 8:13 and we are somewhere near Rochester, New York. In spite of the early hour, it seems like we've been traveling half a day already. I guess we have been on the road since about 1:40 this morning. That is about six and a half hours.

Wayne Troyer is playing with his new GPS and just now informed us that we are 996 miles from Florida. He just got it a day or two ago because he had the bad luck of having their boat tip over and the GPS that he had along went sailing on down the river without him.

Our driver is about six feet tall and skinny. He is wearing a denim shirt and denim jeans and cowboy boots and a black cowboy hat with a gaudy red handkerchief for a hatband. He has a real beard and mustache, not one of those ugly goatee things.

12:47

Well, we are in Canada at last, after fiddling around in customs for about half an hour. Anyway, we got through, and here we are sailing northeast on 401 to the beat of a Blackhawk CD.

This morning it was raining now and then, but right now the sky is filled with fleecy fair weather clouds, the sky is blue, and the sun shines down between the clouds.

We got to St. Michel des Saints at about 5:15, after being on the road for a little over sixteen hours. Now that was a long day, especially since most of us got only two hours of sleep or less last night.

Until about sixty miles from here the country we passed through was pretty flat. Some of it was covered with forest and some was farmland. Once we started getting farther north it got rougher, with some pretty steep and tall hills rising up from the flat valleys below. It is very scenic.

Oh, I forgot to make mention of the numerous little lakes that we passed. Most of them were as blue as the sky above and looked just like a picture in a travel advertisement.

Tuesday, June 10, 2003; 5:58 A.M.

I woke up about half an hour ago and saw that the sun was shining in the corner of the window, so I looked at my watch—5:29 A.M.! The sun had cleared the horizon just a few minutes earlier.

11:28 P.M.

Well, here we are with one evening of bear hunting under our belts. They all saw bears except me. That might have been because I dropped one of my gloves after getting up on the stand and was constantly fidgeting, trying to keep those darn mosquitoes at bay. I tell you, they were positively murderous! I never saw such things before. By the time we got back to camp my ears were covered with blood and dried mosquitoes.

The only things that came to my bait were the squirrels that ran past it and the snowshoe hare that came to nibble at the leftover corn.

Harry and Wayne are ready to go fishing. They must be hard up to go fishing at this time of the night. Just now Harry said that he once heard that pike either bite or they don't bite. Hmmmm ... I think there was more to it, but I'm not sure what.

The others did a little better with their bear hunting though. Harry shot at one, but missed completely. Wayne saw one (probably the one that charged the outfitter on Saturday), but it didn't come close enough for him to get a shot at it. Willis had a sow with three cubs under his tree. While we were hanging Wayne's stand we heard a crash in the underbrush not far off, but we did not see anything. The outfitter even looked a little scared. But we had his hatchet along, just in case a bear would act unruly, but so far none did. He wants at least two of us to walk in and out to and from the stand with whoever hunts there.

No doubt about it, there are bears around here. There are bear droppings everywhere.

Wednesday, June 11, 2003; 8:07 A.M.

It's raining, it's raining, it's raining once again ... It's about 50° this morning. I was thinking about putting on my rain gear and going fishing, but I haven't gotten that far yet.

The road to the cabin is truly a road less traveled. It is wide enough to let a vehicle pass through, but that is about it. The last few miles are definitely 4WD only. It wouldn't be so bad if we didn't have to go back and forth every evening to get to our bear hunting stands.

Doesn't seem like Wayne and Harry caught any fish 'cause Wayne says there are no fish in this lake.

Reuben fished all evening and caught nothing, and saw only a few fish on his fish-finder.

Friday, June 13, 2003; 7:39 A.M.

Just woke up a few minutes ago. No wonder either. We worked till 2:00 last night filleting fish and hanging our two bears on the rafters of the front porch.

Yesterday was an absolutely perfect day for fishing—blue skies, 60 or 70°, and between the six of us we caught 28 pike, of which four were larger than 30 inches. We caught them all at Lac Pouele, which is about two miles from the cabin.

Now for the bear stories—they are WILD!

Wednesday evening

I am sitting in my tree stand waiting for a bear to come along. So far I haven't seen any yet. The mosquitoes and blackflies are enough to drive a body nuts. I am wearing a baseball cap with a head net over it. Last night the head net drooped down against my ears and the mosquitoes could sit on it and sting my ears through the net, so today I found some wire behind the cabin and made a little brim to prop the net away from my head. I taped it on with duct tape and now the mosquitoes can't get my ears.

Suddenly a bear appears through the brush not far away. He fiddles around just out of sight (the brush is very thick around here) for a long time, maybe fifteen minutes. My heart races and slows down again. He comes in sniffing around and goes back out again, comes back in, starts eating, goes away, sits down for a few seconds, then starts back in again, dragging his rear end the first few steps. I draw, but no good shot presents itself, so I let down again. I am shaking so much that the tip of my arrow is dancing and it's a wonder the mosquitoes sitting on it don't fall off. He goes away and lies down for perhaps fifteen minutes. He comes back and takes a few bites. Suddenly he looks around, then takes off down the woods at a decent clip. A minute or so later another bear appears and fiddles around a while. Finally he comes back and starts eating. I draw again, but then he starts walking away. I don't want to shoot while he's moving, so I let down again. He comes back and pulls a small bag of meat scraps out of the gunny sack and, like a little boy in a cookie jar, takes it and runs to a spot ten yards from my tree and sits there eating it, slurping noisily all the time. The brush and branches are so thick that I can't get a good shot, so I sit there and watch him.

When Danny and Reuben come to pick me up I start talking and hollering, but the bear stays right there. I shoot an arrow into the ground eight feet behind him. He never bats an eye. I start down the tree. Halfway down I see him sitting there ten yards away, looking at me, so I climb back up. I holler at Danny and Reuben to go get Harry and come back and chase him away. After what seemed like a fairly long time they return. Harry grabs a pickax, Danny a shovel, and Reuben a spotlight. They chase him away and we go back out to the truck.

Harry shot at one and is not sure whether he hit it or not. Wayne has hit one. We find where Harry's arrow hit a birch log that had been lying over the bait. Looks like a clean miss.

We track Wayne's bear till the game tracker string stops where it was torn off. There is a not much of a blood trail. Finally that too runs out and we go back to the cabin.

This afternoon we went fishing in Lac Pouele. We caught two pike (I think it was two) at the far end of the lake. Another one made off with my only big Rapala. When we were ready to go back, our trolling motor battery seemed a little weak. By the time we had gone a fourth of the way back, it was totally dead. We didn't have any oars along, so I cast my lure into the brush along the shore and pulled us in. We got a few poles, and with them and a large fish net as a paddle we started back toward the landing. Finally we went back to shore and sent Willis and Reuben back to fetch a fresh battery. Wayne and I got tired of waiting and poled, paddled, and somehow propelled the boat back to the landing. By this time the others were down the woods with a battery, so Wayne got a fresh battery and motored down to fetch them and the other boat (we had been towing one boat all afternoon).

Thursday forenoon

We are out on Lac Pouele fishing for pike. the sun is shining, the sky is clear, and the temperature is in the sixties I would guess—perfect for fishing!

We ended that outing with 28 pike in our coolers, ranging from 23 to 32 inches long.

Several of the pike followed the lure back to the boat and we saw them grab the lure and go with it. Now that is pretty exciting fishing!

Thursday evening

I am heading for my stand. I am just about there when a black form crashes away with a "WOOF!" It doesn't go very far. I think I see it watching me. I start up the tree with my hatchet in one hand and my bow in the other. Somehow I reach the stand without dropping anything. I put everything in order and sit down. After a while the bear starts circling around and comes in right under my tree. He sniffs around the base of my tree. I hope he won't decide to come up. He turns and heads for the bait. I draw. A few feet from the bait he pauses. Whock! an arrow thuds into the ground beside him. He jumps to one side and stands there. I nock another arrow, draw, and WHOCK! I see it sticking out of his left shoulder. He barrels up the woods about forty yards and starts moaning. It sounds awful, but I know he is dead. I wait a while, then follow him. He lies there, dead as a doornail. By eight o'clock he is out by the trail waiting for the ride home. Harry thinks he has hit one and that he heard it moaning, so we know he has made a good shot. We run over and fetch Wayne, who hasn't seen anything. We follow Harry's game tracker string and find a good-sized bear at the end of it, quite a bit larger than mine. We snap a few pictures, gut it, and drag it out to the truck. As we start, Wayne heads off down the woods away from the truck. I look at my compass and tell him which way the truck is. He says without a compass he would probably have ended up in Florida!

When we reach the truck the lights are still on! In our haste to go get Harry's bear the driver forgot to turn them off. He tries to start the engine, but the weak battery just doesn't quite do it anymore. He waits a few moments and tries again, not really expecting much to happen. Vroom! It starts! What a welcome sound!

Willis saw the sow again, but didn't get a shot.

When we get back to the cabin there are a mess of pike waiting to be filleted. We get done at about two A.M. and by two thirty I am in bed.

Friday morning

The others go fishing for pike in Lac Pouele. They catch half a dozen (Danny caught three). He was pretty tickled.

Harry and I stay home and butcher our bears, after snapping some photos of them hanging on the porch of the cabin.

Friday evening

Danny and Reuben went to town to get ice and freezer bags. But first they dropped off the bear hunters. Willis took Harry's stand and climbed a tree near the bait. I sat in Willis' stand with a camera and my good old hatchet.

For a long time nothing happened. We dozed off now and then. Willis once nearly dropped his bow, but caught it just in time.

I had nearly given up seeing anything when a stick cracked in the woods behind me. Slowly I turned my head to look and there was the sow with cubs. Willis drew his bow, but there were no good shots at the bear so he let down again. The bears turned and started away, then turned and came back again. I didn't dare look around for fear they would see me and be spooked. This time Willis put an arrow through her. She gave a startled grunt as it hit, then she ran off into the woods grunting at nearly every step.

We headed back out to the road and waited till the others came back, then we tried to track her down. The game tracker string was torn off after about fifty yards, but there was a pretty good blood trail. We followed that for about an hour and about three hundred yards. We thought we heard her running off, so we decided to go back home and wait till tomorrow morning to follow her.

Saturday morning

We followed the trail a little farther, but it rained a little last night and it was pretty tough to find. Finally we gave it up and went trout fishing.

We had tied the boat at the cabin on top of the truck to take along to the trout lake (Lac Savanne). We went past Gerry Risser's camp en route and stopped to talk a few moments. I don't think he really liked seeing the boat on top of the truck.

When we got to Savanne, there were already four boats there. Willis, Reuben, and I took one, and Harry and Wayne took another. The fishing was not too hot. Wayne caught several (only one keeper), and Reuben caught one that was about the size of the big Rapalas we had been using on pike. It looked rather comical. We got our lures snagged innumerable times and Reuben's reel handle fell off, so we went back to shore. It was drizzling and the fish weren't biting, so we started back to the cabin. Danny wasn't feeling too well, and we wanted him to get plenty of rest so that he could drive home tomorrow. We took a different road on the way home to save some miles. About halfway through we came upon a bad washout with a few skinny birch logs thrown across. It would have supported a four-wheeler but no truck! Not much to do but turn around and go back the way we came.

Wayne and Willis went hunting again, and Harry and I went birding until the mosquitoes chased us back.

Willis had one bear coming in, but he was unaware of it until he moved his hand to chase away some mosquitoes, and as he did so something went crashing off into the brush. Likely a bear.

When we got to Wayne's stand, he told us that he had been charged on his way in. It was an old mama with young ones. She took one look at him and came for him at a run. He stood his ground, and she stopped about five feet away, turned, and disappeared into the brush. But "she" was only a grouse! No bears.

Sunday forenoon

When we got back to the cabin last night, we had to pack our bags and load the truck so as to be ready for an early start this morning. When that was done I showered for the first time since leaving town on Tuesday. Got to bed probably around 2:00 A.M.

By 6:35 A.M. we were bumping our way out the old two-track for the last time. It took forty-five minutes to go the first nine miles.

We registered our bears at a little place where the woman could barely speak English.

I had never met these guys until they picked me up Monday morning at 2:00 A.M. We had a blast, and by the end of the week we knew each other quite well!

Legendary Adventures

Elk Hunting Story

WAYNE MAST · *Fryburg, Ohio*

September 20, 2004

WE'VE JUST GOT done eating breakfast and filling the truck and we're cruising west on I-90. Yeeaa!! Hooray for Montana!!

September 20

Just got to the hotel from Cabela's and are ready to hit the sack.

September 22

Well, I saw my first elk. Leroy spotted a couple of elk way up on the mountain, so we stopped and looked them over. There were seven cows, maybe eight, and a nice big 6 x 6 bull. They were on a little finger ridge that was so steep you'd think their legs must be shorter on the uphill side!

September 23, Thursday

We got our stuff together yesterday afternoon and drove over to the trailhead this morning. It was too late to pack in today, so we rode up an old trail towards Lake Mountain. We saw a couple deer up near the peak and a black bear on a slide half a mile away. Leroy tried to stalk the bear, but it moved down into the timber and he couldn't find it anymore.

Friday we packed in to our hunting area and set up camp in a small flat beside the Blackfoot River.

Saturday we hunted, but I didn't see much game. I spent part of the afternoon sitting on top of the Continental Divide gazing at scenery too awe-inspiring to even begin describing.

Leroy found a dead bull elk up Dobrota Creek that was covered with brush and leaves. Bear? Probably.

Sunday we loafed around and filled our stomachs! All that hiking sure whets the appetite! For supper Saturday evening I had a can of chili with a box of Rice-a-Roni with some other vegetables mixed in, altogether about twice as much as I could eat back home.

Monday I hunted up Tobacco Valley a couple miles. I stopped to watch a squirrel, and as I started off again a twig snapped close by. I caught a glimpse of brown fur and my first thought was lion. Then I got a better look and saw it was only a coyote. He was gone before I got a shot, but I dropped him a minute later as he leaped onto the trunk of a fallen tree and stood there looking the other way.

That evening I got to camp early and climbed the ridge and glassed till sunset. I saw several elk and muleys, all several miles away.

Monday evening Abe returned to camp with glowing tales of big bucks on the ridge west of Cooney Creek, so he and I both hunted up there the next morning. I saw a couple does and several decent bucks but none were really huge. Not long after they crossed the ridge out of sight, Abe killed one of them with one shot in the back of the head at 350 yards. The deer tumbled down the slope a dozen yards or so and ended up with an antler broken loose, either from the bullet or the tumble. It was a nice 3x3, about 15 to 16 inches wide.

Abe fetched one of the horses and packed the whole carcass down to camp. I don't know how he got her down there, but it looked awful steep from where I was. When he got to camp he noticed that his tag was no longer on the deer. Uh-oh. One of the outfitter's men found it that evening and brought it over to our camp the next day.

I spent the rest of the day up there on the rocky, windswept ridge top. I took a noontime nap in a grassy crevice in the rock. I saw some more deer and elk, but they were all over on the next ridge a mile or two away. Camp was in plain sight and less than a mile away, but it took me an hour to get there.

Wednesday morning I helped Abe bone his deer and hang it up in a tree.

Once that was done I hiked up the ridge behind camp toward Kome Mt. I saw Abe and a couple does on the way back.

Thursday morning I went up that way again. I saw two deer in a meadow below Evans Peak and tried to stalk them, but by the time I got halfway there the clouds lowered down around me till I couldn't see more than about fifty yards, so I headed back to camp earlier than usual.

Friday Raymond and I both hunted the area below Evans Peak.

On my way up I saw some black bear tracks in the trail. I proceeded rather quietly and cautiously after that, especially through the brush across Eagle Creek where visibility was almost measured by inches at times!

It was beautiful up there, but it was cold. The fog blowing up over the ridge the night before had left a thick coating of hoarfrost on the upwind side of every tree and bush and rock, so thick in places that it dropped off in little piles like snow.

Mid-morning I met the scrawny young guide and his hunter and talked with them a bit. The guide was from Pittsburgh and the hunter from Vermont. They said they had seen a record book muley up on Evans Peak that morning.

I fiddled around on the ridge till mid-afternoon. I met Raymond and was talking with him when I looked around and saw Leroy coming down the ridge toward us.

Toward evening Leroy headed up toward Evans Peak. We watched a while, then I headed down around the bare, rocky backside of the ridge to watch the meadow. I looked and looked and waited and looked, but no deer was there to see.

Later I saw a couple bucks scattered across the east face of the peak, grazing in the little brush patches.

The sun was still a few minutes above the horizon and dropping fast. Camp was three miles away as the crow flies and a good five miles and two hours as we "fly." I got up to head toward camp and turned for one last look up at the face of Evans Peak. As I did so some vague notion inspired me to follow Leroy up the mountain instead of toward camp. I scrambled up the ridge and across the face toward the ridge on the far side of the face. I glassed the flat, brushy south face of the peak, but not a hair could I see. Leroy was nowhere in sight and I disgustedly started down the south face, sliding, jumping, scooting, whatever. I hadn't gone far when I saw a patch of orange which was Leroy. He stood above a patch of brush glassing the meadow below. He motioned frantically for me to hurry down and I did so, as quietly as possible. Half a dozen cows and calves and one bull were grazing in a meadow three or four hundred yards below. I slipped and slithered, in plain sight of the cows, down the hill to the next patch of brush, then frantically dug out my binocs to make sure the bull was legal. The binocular lenses were fogged shut and I couldn't see a thing! I grabbed my handkerchief, wiped the lenses off, and looked hurriedly for brow tines, but it was so far and the light was fading, so I could barely see his antlers. Finally he moved his head and I saw long brow tines silhouetted against the light tan of his back. I slipped down around the patch of brush to a fallen tree about the right height for a rifle rest, but then the bull was behind a tree! I slithered farther down the hill to where there was a clear shot, but there the tree was so thin its use as a rest was rather dubious. Well, I shot anyway. The cows ran off, but the bull still stood there. I shot again and the dust flew from a rock beside the bull. Another shot and he tumbled down the hill like a chunk of rock, coming to rest against a small tree. I had one shot left, so I fired again for insurance.

I hurried down the hill as fast as I could (not all that fast, as the hill was nearly 45 degrees and jagged bare rock in places), telling Leroy to bring my pack. He had to climb back up a ways to get it, and as he drew near, the pack started rolling down the hill toward him!

The bull was a 4x4, 29 inches wide inside, no record breaker, but it was my first elk and I was satisfied with it.

After admiring the bull we dragged it down the hill to a slightly more level spot and started boning. By now it was completely dark. About half-way through we heard something rustling, and I thought I saw eyes in the brush nearby. We hollered a time or two, but nothing moved. Leroy got his .300 Weatherby and we started toward the noise. We felt rather foolish when we realized it was the foil space blanket rustling in the breeze! We had placed the meat on the blanket to keep the dirt off.

It was 10:30 P.M. when we got done boning and started toward camp. Both of us were out of water and very thirsty and oh my, the first gurgling little brook we came to sounded quite wonderful indeed! I don't think I ever appreciated a drink of water quite as much as I did that one!

We were nearing the river when I saw a large animal coming down the main trail toward the trail we were on. At first I thought it was a horse, then we saw it was a big brown bear. It wasn't as huge as the grizzly we saw later, just big, probably a brown black bear. We hollered at him, and kept on hollering. He stopped, looked a while, turned, and ran up the way he had come, which was also the way we were headed! Leroy had his .300 Weatherby ready and I had my .30/06 and the pepper spray handy the rest of the way back!

Saturday morning the scrawny guide from Pennsylvania and his hunter rode up to our camp and informed us that Abe's deer was gone. We got our guns and went to investigate and, sure enough, it was all gone. All that was left were a few scraps of rope and some claw marks on the tree. The guide's horses didn't even want to go past the place where the deer had been. They probably still smelled the bear.

One of the deer's antlers, which had broken off as it rolled down the hill, was back in camp, so Abe still has half a muley rack, without a tag on it.

On the way up the mountain to fetch the meat, the old lunatic Raymond was riding started acting up. I can't recall what capers she pulled, but one time she went tearing down the slope with the saddlebags flapping and flying. By the time she stopped, quivering from head to foot, Raymond's Swarovski binoculars had flown out of the saddlebags and were lying a couple inches from her hind foot!

We broke camp that evening, but left the tents, sleeping bags, etc. hanging in a tree and packed out only the meat and antlers. It was 2:00 A.M. Sunday morning when we got to Raymond's house and hit the sack.

Sunday we ate a huge breakfast and loafed around all day.

Monday we stocked up on supplies and in the afternoon we went salmon snagging in the Swan River.

Tuesday we packed in again and set up camp.

Wednesday morning Leroy and I both headed up towards Evans Peak again. I sat up there on the ridge for awhile, alternately glassing and sleeping. Early in the afternoon Leroy appeared on the ridge just north of Evans, whereupon I gathered my stuff and headed in that direction too.

I was still climbing up the rocks on the back side of the ridge when a shot rang out from the Lee's big .300 Weatherby. As I topped the ridge I saw two big bucks walking along the skyline on the next ridge. I put the thick part of the crosshairs on the one deer's back and fired. They still stood there so I held a foot or two higher and fired again. One of the deer went over the ridge out of sight and the other one came back down into the green brush patches where they had bedded. I thought he walked just a little bit funny and thought he might be hit, so I decided to go and check it out. I went down the slope a ways, and came up toward him from below, where the brush hid my approach. But it hid him too. I was crawling through the brush, and as I came out into an opening looking uphill, I heard the thud of feet going downhill. I looked around just in time to see him disappear into the brush below me. I ran downhill to where I could see most of the area immediately below me. Finally I spotted him, and sent another shot that way. I thought I saw him rolling and hurried on down. And then I saw him again, shot too hastily and missed, shot again, and that was it. One of my first two shots had hit him in the gut just behind the diaphragm. Was I ever glad I followed him up!

Most of you have heard of the term "ground shrinkage." Well, this deer didn't suffer from it. In fact, he looked larger at close range than he had in the distance.

He fell headfirst into a patch of brush, and he was so heavy I couldn't pull him back up. I had to cut away some of the brush below him and drag him down the hill a ways to an old stump, which kept him from rolling on down the hill. It was still neccessary to tie his legs to the brush above to keep him from slipping around the stump and go crashing down the slope.

It took about two hours or so to get him boned and everything.

Leroy was finished boning his buck and found me before I was quite done. Once I was finished we started over toward the elk kill to see if anything had been cleaning it up. I guess something had! We were several hundred feet above the kill site on a small promontory glassing the meadow below when a huge gray-brown grizzly came walking up the slope through the pines straight to the elk kill site. And it was enormous! Its head must have been a foot and a half wide! I was rather alarmed, not about us, but about the meat of the two deer a quarter mile above us that would have to lie there till morning. Well, we couldn't shoot the bear, so we moved the meat from my deer a couple hundred yards away from the kill site and hoped the bear wouldn't find it. Leroy's deer was already way up the mountain and was as safe there as it would be if we moved it.

On the way back to camp I said something to Lee about this making a good story to tell around the campfire sometime. "Yes," he said, "if the griz doesn't get us first!"

Next morning the others went hunting again. I saddled Rocko and Patty and headed for Evans to fetch the meat. Leroy met me up there about noon and helped get the meat and heads loaded on the packhorses. Surprisingly to me, the meat was untouched, so the grizzly was either full or hadn't smelled the deer.

This time we hung the meat well away from any trees and eight or ten feet up, and it was still there when we were ready to pack out on Saturday.

After I left Lee, he went after a bull he had spotted down in the Cabin Creek drainage. He never did see it after he got down to where it had been and returned without it.

Friday I was going to accompany Abe over into Cabin Creek, down behind Evans. About halfway up the ridge behind camp my enthusiasm kind of died away and disappeared. I gave him my GPS and spent the rest of the day loafing around up there on the ridge, glassing, sleeping, and soaking up the sun.

That evening several dippers were singing in the river when I went to get our jug of milk, which we kept in the icy water. The dippers are little gray birds about the size of a starling, and they wade out into the icy water chasing bugs and who knows what else. It almost made me shiver to watch them!

Saturday morning we broke camp and packed out. Abe and I led the packhorses, and Raymond and Leroy rode the other two out. It was 15 miles from camp to the trailhead and it took us five and a half hours to get there. Needless to say, we were ready sit down and relax when we reached the trailhead.

Monday morning we headed for Glacier National Park. It was cloudy and we couldn't see the peaks, but what we could see was well worth the drive—huge valleys, rugged cliffs, glaciers, small valleys, rock slide slopes—it is beautiful scenery, but it is not exactly the most hospitable terrain around.

At Many Glacier several sheep and goats were grazing on a ridge visible from the parking lot.

On the way back to St. Ignatius we took St. Rt. 2 around the south end of the park. It is a very lonely road that reminds me of some of the crooked little back roads in southern Holmes County, Ohio, that twist and turn and rise and fall seemingly without rhyme or reason or destination.

Tuesday evening we went to the neighbors for supper. When we arrived they had a pair of huge binocs set up on a tripod. With them we spotted a herd of goats on top of a high ridge in the Mission Mountains to the east. We got out a topographic map and figured out these goats were six miles away!

Wednesday we toured the Bison Range, a huge fenced-in preserve just west of St. Ignatius. We saw several buffalo, some elk, muleys, antelope, and a couple coyotes. One of the elk and several of the muleys were big and one of the deer was positively enormous.

There is a road winding through the preserve, and at one point it comes out on top of the ridge and suddenly confronts you with a view of the twelve-mile-wide valley and the snowcapped Mission Range towering on the other side. It is one of those places where you could sit and just look for a long, long time.

We were in no hurry to get home. We spent part of two days hunting pheasants and partridge on several different ranches. If my memory is correct, we managed to kill one pheasant, which fell to a lucky shot from my gun.

One afternoon we went looking for prairie dogs. We shot a couple, and

Legendary Adventures

all the shooting scared a bobcat out of a nearby patch of brush.

The following excerpt from one of my favorite poems was written about the Far North, Alaska and the Yukon, but it expresses some of my feelings about the West, especially the very last line!

> I've stood in some mighty-mouthed hollow
> That's plumb-full of hush to the brim;
> I've watched the big, husky sun wallow
> In crimson and gold, and grow dim,
> Till the moon set the pearly peaks gleaming,
> And the stars tumbled out, neck and crop;
> And I've thought that I surely was dreaming,
> With the peace o' the world piled on top.
>
> The summer — no sweeter was ever;
> The sunshiny woods all athrill;
> The grayling aleap in the river,
> The bighorn asleep on the hill.
> The strong life that never knows harness;
> The wilds where the caribou call;
> The freshness, the freedom, the farness —
> O God! how I'm stuck on it all...
>
> There's a land where the mountains are nameless,
> And the rivers all run who knows where...
>
> There's a land — oh, it beckons and beckons,
> And I want to go back — and I will.

from The Spell of the Yukon by Robert Service

The Best Shot in History

(LEGENDARY TALE)

NOW FOLKS, IF you jest set back and have a spell, and I'll jest go ahead and share a tale that happened to me many moons ago in Mud Creek Canyon in the no man's land. Ya'll know that fellers say that they can shoot pretty good with their guns, "them there rifles." Ha, I tell you, I am the best on this side of the mountain and I use them muzzleloaders, the type of gun you make your own load of lead, you know.

I haven't been huntin' for years and I'll tell you why. The last time I went hunting I had so much luck, my luck bag didn't hold it all. It spoiled the twang in hunting.

I had gone out to see if I can't bag a nice deer. So the first game I saw was a huge bear with beady red eyes staring at me. So with shaking knees I pulled my trusty muzzleloader to my shoulders. I fired and killed the bear. As my rifle cracked, thru the smoke I saw a flutter in the trees to my left near the creek, while to my right I heard a thrashing in the bushes.

When I got to my bear that squared a 14' rug, I found my bullet had gone thru it, and struck an edge of a rock and split it in two. Half of the bullet had taken an upward turn, asplit a limb where two wild turkeys had been roosting. The split limb had caught their toes like a trap.

After skinning the bear and dressing the turkeys, and hanging my prizes in the tree, I proceeded to follow the other half of the bullet. I found it had struck and killed a big 10-point buck, passed entirely thru it,

189

and hit a hollow oak tree beyond the creek, and honey was pouring from it in a golden stream. I hurriedly dressed the deer and hung it to my other trophies, and crossed the creek to the tree that appeared pretty sweet to me. In my haste, while crossing the creek, I stepped into a deep hole that was deeper than me, 'cause finally after paddling frantically and getting myself on shore, I felt a flopping. Sitting down to catch my breath I pulled off my boots and got six nice trout out of each one.

As I put my prize on the stringer, two rabbits being chased by a fox darted into my boots for cover. So I grabbed a club lying near me, knocked the daylights out of the fox, and a tap on my boots finished the hares.

Having no use for the club, I hurled it into the bush and scattered a covey of feeding quail, while killing eight.

Then as I raised my hands high to give thanks for such a wonderful hunt, my hands closed on the legs of four ducks flying by. Completely overcome, I knelt down for a prayer of thankfulness and found myself moving slowly along on the back of a big turtle.

That's right, I haven't been hunting since 'cause I know you can't beat my record—1 bear, 2 turkeys, 1 deer, 12 trout, 2 rabbits, 1 fox, 8 quail, 4 ducks, and 1 turtle—with one shot.

The Dumb and Dumber

(LEGENDARY TALE)

ONE DAY WHILE hunting, this hunter came upon two hunters dragging a nice 8-pointer out of the woods by the hind leg. The experienced hunter greeted them and congratulated them for the luck they had on their hunt.

It was apparent the two fellows were somewhat new to the hunting game, because they described how much work it was dragging this deer out of the woods backwards. It was snagging brush and all, and its head just whipped around.

So the experienced hunter advised them that it would be easier if they both would go and grab one side of the antlers; that way the deer would drag easier. WOW! They thanked the guy for the tip and continued their trek. The experienced hunter continued his walk to his stand with a smile on his face.

Well, an hour later the one hunter looked over to his partner and exclaimed how easy it was dragging the deer, and how lucky they were to have met the experienced hunter, and how really elated he was on their progress. The other hunter agreed that it was much easier, but said he thought they were getting farther and farther away from the truck!

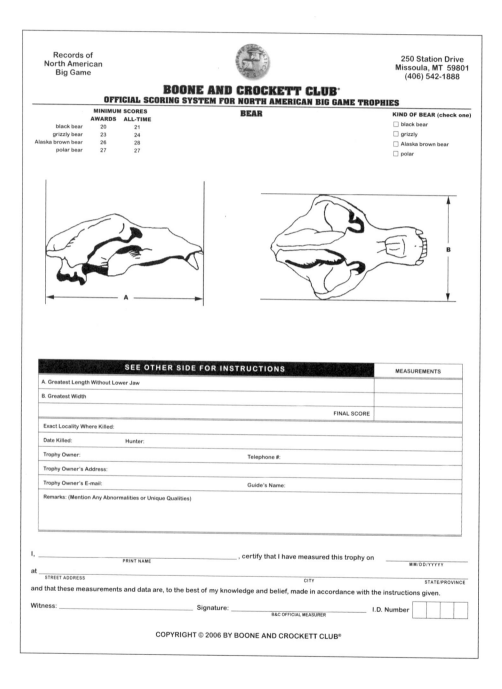

Records of
North American
Big Game

250 Station Drive
Missoula, MT 59801
(406) 542-1888

BOONE AND CROCKETT CLUB®
OFFICIAL SCORING SYSTEM FOR NORTH AMERICAN BIG GAME TROPHIES

BEAR

	MINIMUM SCORES	
	AWARDS	ALL-TIME
black bear	20	21
grizzly bear	23	24
Alaska brown bear	26	28
polar bear	27	27

KIND OF BEAR (check one)
- ☐ black bear
- ☐ grizzly
- ☐ Alaska brown bear
- ☐ polar

SEE OTHER SIDE FOR INSTRUCTIONS	MEASUREMENTS
A. Greatest Length Without Lower Jaw	
B. Greatest Width	
FINAL SCORE	

Exact Locality Where Killed:

Date Killed: Hunter:

Trophy Owner: Telephone #:

Trophy Owner's Address:

Trophy Owner's E-mail: Guide's Name:

Remarks: (Mention Any Abnormalities or Unique Qualities)

I, _____ , certify that I have measured this trophy on _____
         PRINT NAME   MM/DD/YYYYY

at _____ _____ _____
      STREET ADDRESS   CITY   STATE/PROVINCE

and that these measurements and data are, to the best of my knowledge and belief, made in accordance with the instructions given.

Witness: _____ Signature: _____ I.D. Number ☐☐☐☐
                                              B&C OFFICIAL MEASURER

INSTRUCTIONS FOR MEASURING BEAR

Measurements are taken with calipers or by using parallel perpendiculars, to the nearest **one-sixteenth** of an inch, without reduction of fractions. Official measurements cannot be taken until the skull has air dried for at least 60 days after the animal was killed. All adhering flesh, membrane and cartilage must be completely removed **before** official measurements are taken.

A. Greatest Length is measured between perpendiculars parallel to the long axis of the skull, without the lower jaw and excluding malformations.

B. Greatest Width is measured between perpendiculars at right angles to the long axis.

ENTRY AFFIDAVIT FOR ALL HUNTER-TAKEN TROPHIES

For the purpose of entry into the Boone and Crockett Club's® records, North American big game harvested by the use of the following methods or under the following conditions are ineligible:

I. Spotting or herding game from the air, followed by landing in its vicinity for the purpose of pursuit and shooting;
II. Herding or chasing with the aid of any motorized equipment;
III. Use of electronic communication devices to guide hunters to game, artificial lighting, electronic light intensifying devices (night vision optics), sights with built-in electronic range-finding capabilities, thermal imaging equipment, electronic game calls or cameras/timers/motion tracking devices that transmit images and other information to the hunter;
IV. Confined by artificial barriers, including escape-proof fenced enclosures;
V. Transplanted for the purpose of commercial shooting;
VI. By the use of traps or pharmaceuticals;
VII. While swimming, helpless in deep snow, or helpless in any other natural or artificial medium;
VIII. On another hunter's license;
IX. Not in full compliance with the game laws or regulations of the federal government or of any state, province, territory, or tribal council on reservations or tribal lands;

Please answer the following questions:

Were dogs used in conjunction with the pursuit and harvest of this animal?
☐ Yes ☐ No

If the answer to the above question is yes, answer the following statements:

1. I was present on the hunt at the times the dogs were released to pursue this animal.
☐ True ☐ False

2. If electronic collars were attached to any of the dogs, receivers were not used to harvest this animal.
☐ True ☐ False

To the best of my knowledge the answers to the above statements are true. If the answer to either #1 or #2 above is false, please explain on a separate sheet.

I certify that the trophy scored on this chart was not taken in violation of the conditions listed above. In signing this statement, I understand that if the information provided on this entry is found to be misrepresented or fraudulent in any respect, it will not be accepted into the Awards Program and 1) all of my prior entries are subject to deletion from future editions of **Records of North American Big Game** 2) future entries may not be accepted.

FAIR CHASE, as defined by the Boone and Crockett Club®, is the ethical, sportsmanlike and lawful pursuit and taking of any free-ranging wild, native North American big game animal in a manner that does not give the hunter an improper advantage over such game animals.

The Boone and Crockett Club® may exclude the entry of any animal that it deems to have been taken in an unethical manner or under conditions deemed inappropriate by the Club.

Date: _____ Signature of Hunter: _____
(SIGNATURE MUST BE WITNESSED BY AN OFFICIAL MEASURER OR A NOTARY PUBLIC.)

Date: _____ Signature of Notary or Official Measurer: _____

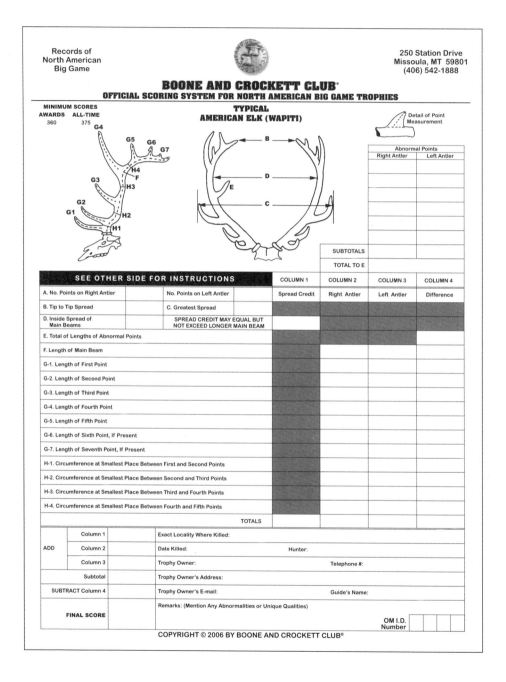

SEE OTHER SIDE FOR INSTRUCTIONS

			COLUMN 1	COLUMN 2	COLUMN 3	COLUMN 4
A. No. Points on Right Antler		No. Points on Left Antler	Spread Credit	Right Antler	Left Antler	Difference
B. Tip to Tip Spread		C. Greatest Spread				
D. Inside Spread of Main Beams		SPREAD CREDIT MAY EQUAL BUT NOT EXCEED LONGER MAIN BEAM				
E. Total of Lengths of Abnormal Points						
F. Length of Main Beam						
G-1. Length of First Point						
G-2. Length of Second Point						
G-3. Length of Third Point						
G-4. Length of Fourth Point						
G-5. Length of Fifth Point						
G-6. Length of Sixth Point, If Present						
G-7. Length of Seventh Point, If Present						
H-1. Circumference at Smallest Place Between First and Second Points						
H-2. Circumference at Smallest Place Between Second and Third Points						
H-3. Circumference at Smallest Place Between Third and Fourth Points						
H-4. Circumference at Smallest Place Between Fourth and Fifth Points						
		TOTALS				

ADD	Column 1		Exact Locality Where Killed:	
	Column 2		Date Killed:	Hunter:
	Column 3		Trophy Owner:	Telephone #:
	Subtotal		Trophy Owner's Address:	
SUBTRACT Column 4			Trophy Owner's E-mail:	Guide's Name:
FINAL SCORE			Remarks: (Mention Any Abnormalities or Unique Qualities)	OM I.D. Number

I, _____, certify that I have measured this trophy on _____
PRINT NAME   MM/DD/YYYYY

at _____
STREET ADDRESS   CITY   STATE/PROVINCE

and that these measurements and data are, to the best of my knowledge and belief, made in accordance with the instructions given.

Witness: _____ Signature: _____ I.D. Number [ ][ ][ ][ ]
                                                B&C OFFICIAL MEASURER

INSTRUCTIONS FOR MEASURING TYPICAL AMERICAN ELK (WAPITI)

All measurements must be made with a 1/4-inch wide flexible steel tape to the nearest one-eighth of an inch. (Note: A flexible steel cable can be used to measure points and main beams only.) Enter fractional figures in eighths, without reduction. Official measurements cannot be taken until the antlers have air dried for at least 60 days after the animal was killed.

A. Number of Points on Each Antler: To be counted a point, the projection must be at least one inch long, with length exceeding width at one inch or more of length. All points are measured from tip of point to nearest edge of beam as illustrated. Beam tip is counted as a point but not measured as a point. **Point totals do not add into the final score.**

B. Tip to Tip Spread is measured between tips of main beams. **Tip to tip spread does not add into the final score.**

C. Greatest Spread is measured between perpendiculars at a right angle to the center line of the skull at widest part, whether across main beams or points. **Greatest spread does not add into the final score.**

D. Inside Spread of Main Beams is measured at a right angle to the center line of the skull at widest point between main beams. Enter this measurement again as the Spread Credit if it is less than or equal to the length of the longer main beam; if greater, enter longer main beam length for Spread Credit.

E. Total of Lengths of all Abnormal Points: Abnormal Points are those non-typical in location (such as points originating from a point or from bottom or sides of main beam) or pattern (extra points, not generally paired). Measure in usual manner and record in appropriate blanks.

F. Length of Main Beam is measured from the center of the lowest outside edge of burr over the outer side to the most distant point of the main beam. The point of beginning is that point on the burr where the center line along the outer side of the beam intersects the burr, then following generally the line of the illustration.

G-1-2-3-4-5-6-7. Length of Normal Points: Normal points project from the top or front of the main beam in the general pattern illustrated. They are measured from nearest edge of main beam over outer curve to tip. Lay the tape along the outer curve of the beam so that the top edge of the tape coincides with the top edge of the beam on both sides of point to determine the baseline for point measurement. Record point length in appropriate blanks.

H-1-2-3-4. Circumferences are taken as detailed in illustration for each measurement.

ENTRY AFFIDAVIT FOR ALL HUNTER-TAKEN TROPHIES

For the purpose of entry into the Boone and Crockett Club's® records, North American big game harvested by the use of the following methods or under the following conditions are ineligible:

I. Spotting or herding game from the air, followed by landing in its vicinity for the purpose of pursuit and shooting;
II. Herding or chasing with the aid of any motorized equipment;
III. Use of electronic communication devices to guide hunters to game, artificial lighting, electronic light intensifying devices (night vision optics), sights with built-in electronic range-finding capabilities, thermal imaging equipment, electronic game calls or cameras/timers/motion tracking devices that transmit images and other information to the hunter;
IV. Confined by artificial barriers, including escape-proof fenced enclosures;
V. Transplanted for the purpose of commercial shooting;
VI. By the use of traps or pharmaceuticals;
VII. While swimming, helpless in deep snow, or helpless in any other natural or artificial medium;
VIII. On another hunter's license;
IX. Not in full compliance with the game laws or regulations of the federal government or of any state, province, territory, or tribal council on reservations or tribal lands;

I certify that the trophy scored on this chart was not taken in violation of the conditions listed above. In signing this statement, I understand that if the information provided on this entry is found to be misrepresented or fraudulent in any respect, it will not be accepted into the Awards Program and 1) all of my prior entries are subject to deletion from future editions of **Records of North American Big Game** 2) future entries may not be accepted.

FAIR CHASE, as defined by the Boone and Crockett Club®, is the ethical, sportsmanlike and lawful pursuit and taking of any free-ranging wild, native North American big game animal in a manner that does not give the hunter an improper advantage over such game animals.

The Boone and Crockett Club® may exclude the entry of any animal that it deems to have been taken in an unethical manner or under conditions deemed inappropriate by the Club.

Date: _____ Signature of Hunter: _____
                              (SIGNATURE MUST BE WITNESSED BY AN OFFICIAL MEASURER OR A NOTARY PUBLIC.)

Date: _____ Signature of Notary or Official Measurer: _____

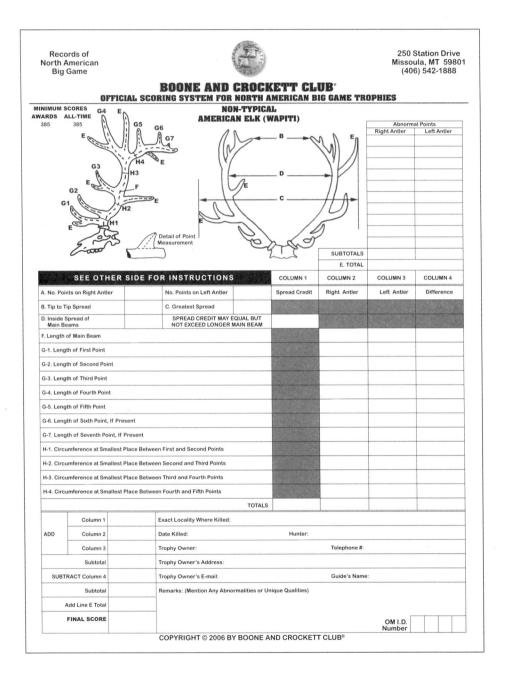

Records of
North American
Big Game

250 Station Drive
Missoula, MT 59801
(406) 542-1888

BOONE AND CROCKETT CLUB®
OFFICIAL SCORING SYSTEM FOR NORTH AMERICAN BIG GAME TROPHIES

NON-TYPICAL AMERICAN ELK (WAPITI)

MINIMUM SCORES	
AWARDS	ALL-TIME
385	385

Abnormal Points	
Right Antler	Left Antler

	SUBTOTALS	
	E. TOTAL	

Detail of Point Measurement

SEE OTHER SIDE FOR INSTRUCTIONS			COLUMN 1	COLUMN 2	COLUMN 3	COLUMN 4
A. No. Points on Right Antler		No. Points on Left Antler	Spread Credit	Right Antler	Left Antler	Difference
B. Tip to Tip Spread		C. Greatest Spread				
D. Inside Spread of Main Beams		SPREAD CREDIT MAY EQUAL BUT NOT EXCEED LONGER MAIN BEAM				
F. Length of Main Beam						
G-1. Length of First Point						
G-2. Length of Second Point						
G-3. Length of Third Point						
G-4. Length of Fourth Point						
G-5. Length of Fifth Point						
G-6. Length of Sixth Point, If Present						
G-7. Length of Seventh Point, If Present						
H-1. Circumference at Smallest Place Between First and Second Points						
H-2. Circumference at Smallest Place Between Second and Third Points						
H-3. Circumference at Smallest Place Between Third and Fourth Points						
H-4. Circumference at Smallest Place Between Fourth and Fifth Points						
		TOTALS				

ADD	Column 1		Exact Locality Where Killed:
	Column 2		Date Killed: Hunter:
	Column 3		Trophy Owner: Telephone #:
	Subtotal		Trophy Owner's Address:
SUBTRACT Column 4			Trophy Owner's E-mail: Guide's Name:
	Subtotal		Remarks: (Mention Any Abnormalities or Unique Qualities)
	Add Line E Total		
	FINAL SCORE		OM I.D. Number

I, _____ , certify that I have measured this trophy on _____
        PRINT NAME   MM/DD/YYYYY

at _____
   STREET ADDRESS   CITY   STATE/PROVINCE

and that these measurements and data are, to the best of my knowledge and belief, made in accordance with the instructions given.

Witness: _____ Signature: _____ I.D. Number ☐ ☐ ☐ ☐
                                                  B&C OFFICIAL MEASURER

INSTRUCTIONS FOR MEASURING NON-TYPICAL AMERICAN ELK (WAPITI)

All measurements must be made with a 1/4-inch wide flexible steel tape to the nearest one-eighth of an inch. (Note: A flexible steel cable can be used to measure points and main beams only.) Enter fractional figures in eighths, without reduction. Official measurements cannot be taken until the antlers have air dried for at least 60 days after the animal was killed.

A. **Number of Points on Each Antler:** To be counted a point, the projection must be at least one inch long, with length exceeding width at one inch or more of length. All points are measured from tip of point to nearest edge of beam as illustrated. Beam tip is counted as a point but not measured as a point. **Point totals do not add into the final score.**

B. **Tip to Tip Spread** is measured between tips of main beams. **Tip to tip spread does not add into the final score.**

C. **Greatest Spread** is measured between perpendiculars at a right angle to the center line of the skull at widest part, whether across main beams or points. **Greatest spread does not add into the final score.**

D. **Inside Spread of Main Beams** is measured at a right angle to the center line of the skull at widest point between main beams. Enter this measurement again as the Spread Credit if it is less than or equal to the length of the longer main beam; if greater, enter longer main beam length for Spread Credit.

E. **Total of Lengths of all Abnormal Points:** Abnormal Points are those non-typical in location (such as points originating from a point or from bottom or sides of main beam) or pattern (extra points, not generally paired). Measure in usual manner and record in appropriate blanks.

F. **Length of Main Beam** is measured from the center of the lowest outside edge of burr over the outer side to the most distant point of the main beam. The point of beginning is that point on the burr where the center line along the outer side of the beam intersects the burr, then following generally the line of the illustration.

G-1-2-3-4-5-6-7. **Length of Normal Points:** Normal points project from the top or front of the main beam in the general pattern illustrated. They are measured from nearest edge of main beam over outer curve to tip. Lay the tape along the outer curve of the beam so that the top edge of the tape coincides with the top edge of the beam on both sides of point to determine the baseline for point measurement. Record point length in appropriate blanks.

H-1-2-3-4. **Circumferences** are taken as detailed in illustration for each measurement.

ENTRY AFFIDAVIT FOR ALL HUNTER-TAKEN TROPHIES

For the purpose of entry into the Boone and Crockett Club's® records, North American big game harvested by the use of the following methods or under the following conditions are ineligible:

I. Spotting or herding game from the air, followed by landing in its vicinity for the purpose of pursuit and shooting;
II. Herding or chasing with the aid of any motorized equipment;
III. Use of electronic communication devices to guide hunters to game, artificial lighting, electronic light intensifying devices (night vision optics), sights with built-in electronic range-finding capabilities, thermal imaging equipment, electronic game calls or cameras/timers/motion tracking devices that transmit images and other information to the hunter;
IV. Confined by artificial barriers, including escape-proof fenced enclosures;
V. Transplanted for the purpose of commercial shooting;
VI. By the use of traps or pharmaceuticals;
VII. While swimming, helpless in deep snow, or helpless in any other natural or artificial medium;
VIII. On another hunter's license;
IX. Not in full compliance with the game laws or regulations of the federal government or of any state, province, territory, or tribal council on reservations or tribal lands;

I certify that the trophy scored on this chart was not taken in violation of the conditions listed above. In signing this statement, I understand that if the information provided on this entry is found to be misrepresented or fraudulent in any respect, it will not be accepted into the Awards Program and 1) all of my prior entries are subject to deletion from future editions of **Records of North American Big Game** 2) future entries may not be accepted.

FAIR CHASE, as defined by the Boone and Crockett Club®, is the ethical, sportsmanlike and lawful pursuit and taking of any free-ranging wild, native North American big game animal in a manner that does not give the hunter an improper advantage over such game animals.

The Boone and Crockett Club® may exclude the entry of any animal that it deems to have been taken in an unethical manner or under conditions deemed inappropriate by the Club.

Date: _____ Signature of Hunter: _____
                                       (SIGNATURE MUST BE WITNESSED BY AN OFFICIAL MEASURER OR A NOTARY PUBLIC.)

Date: _____ Signature of Notary or Official Measurer: _____

197

Legendary Adventures

<table>
<tr><td>Records of
North American
Big Game</td><td></td><td>250 Station Drive
Missoula, MT 59801
(406) 542-1888</td></tr>
</table>

BOONE AND CROCKETT CLUB®
OFFICIAL SCORING SYSTEM FOR NORTH AMERICAN BIG GAME TROPHIES

TYPICAL MULE DEER AND BLACKTAIL DEER

MINIMUM SCORES	AWARDS	ALL-TIME
mule deer	180	190
Columbia blacktail	125	135
Sitka blacktail	100	108

KIND OF DEER (check one)
- ☐ mule deer
- ☐ Columbia blacktail
- ☐ Sitka blacktail

Detail of Point Measurement

Abnormal Points	
Right Antler	Left Antler

SUBTOTALS

TOTAL TO E

SEE OTHER SIDE FOR INSTRUCTIONS

		COLUMN 1	COLUMN 2	COLUMN 3	COLUMN 4
A. No. Points on Right Antler	No. Points on Left Antler	Spread Credit	Right Antler	Left Antler	Difference
B. Tip to Tip Spread	C. Greatest Spread				
D. Inside Spread of Main Beams	SPREAD CREDIT MAY EQUAL BUT NOT EXCEED LONGER MAIN BEAM				
E. Total of Lengths of Abnormal Points					
F. Length of Main Beam					
G-1. Length of First Point, If Present					
G-2. Length of Second Point					
G-3. Length of Third Point, If Present					
G-4. Length of Fourth Point, If Present					
H-1. Circumference at Smallest Place Between Burr and First Point					
H-2. Circumference at Smallest Place Between First and Second Points					
H-3. Circumference at Smallest Place Between Main Beam and Third Point					
H-4. Circumference at Smallest Place Between Second and Fourth Points					
	TOTALS				

ADD	Column 1	Exact Locality Where Killed:
	Column 2	Date Killed: Hunter:
	Column 3	Trophy Owner: Telephone #:
	Subtotal	Trophy Owner's Address:
SUBTRACT Column 4		Trophy Owner's E-mail: Guide's Name:
FINAL SCORE		Remarks: (Mention Any Abnormalities or Unique Qualities)

OM I.D. Number

COPYRIGHT © 2006 BY BOONE AND CROCKETT CLUB®

198

I, _____ , certify that I have measured this trophy on _____
PRINT NAME   MM/DD/YYYYY

at _____
STREET ADDRESS   CITY   STATE/PROVINCE

and that these measurements and data are, to the best of my knowledge and belief, made in accordance with the instructions given.

Witness: _____ Signature: _____ I.D. Number ☐☐☐☐
B&C OFFICIAL MEASURER

INSTRUCTIONS FOR MEASURING TYPICAL MULE AND BLACKTAIL DEER

All measurements must be made with a 1/4-inch wide flexible steel tape to the nearest one-eighth of an inch. (Note: A flexible steel cable can be used to measure points and main beams only.) Enter fractional figures in eighths, without reduction. Official measurements cannot be taken until the antlers have air dried for at least 60 days after the animal was killed.

A. **Number of Points on Each Antler:** To be counted a point, the projection must be at least one inch long, with length exceeding width at one inch or more of length. All points are measured from tip of point to nearest edge of beam. Beam tip is counted as a point but not measured as a point. **Point totals do not add into the final score.**

B. **Tip to Tip Spread** is measured between tips of main beams. **Tip to tip spread does not add into the final score.**

C. **Greatest Spread** is measured between perpendiculars at a right angle to the center line of the skull at widest part, whether across main beams or points. **Greatest spread does not add into the final score.**

D. **Inside Spread of Main Beams** is measured at a right angle to the center line of the skull at widest point between main beams. Enter this measurement again as the Spread Credit **if** it is less than or equal to the length of the longer main beam; if greater, enter longer main beam length for Spread Credit.

E. **Total of Lengths of all Abnormal Points:** Abnormal Points are those non-typical in location such as points originating from a point (exception: G-3 originates from G-2 in perfectly normal fashion) or from bottom or sides of main beam, or any points beyond the normal pattern of five (including beam tip) per antler. Measure each abnormal point in usual manner and enter in appropriate blanks.

F. **Length of Main Beam** is measured from the center of the lowest outside edge of burr over the outer side to the most distant point of the Main Beam. The point of beginning is that point on the burr where the center line along the outer side of the beam intersects the burr, then following generally the line of the illustration.

G-1-2-3-4. **Length of Normal Points:** Normal points are the brow tines and the upper and lower forks as shown in the illustration. They are measured from nearest edge of main beam over outer curve to tip. Lay the tape along the outer curve of the beam so that the top edge of the tape coincides with the top edge of the beam on both sides of point to determine the baseline for point measurement. Record point lengths in appropriate blanks.

H-1-2-3-4. **Circumferences** are taken as detailed in illustration for each measurement. If brow point is missing, take H-1 and H-2 at smallest place between burr and G-2. If G-3 is missing, take H-3 halfway between the base and tip of G-2. If G-4 is missing, take H-4 halfway between G-2 and tip of main beam.

ENTRY AFFIDAVIT FOR ALL HUNTER-TAKEN TROPHIES

For the purpose of entry into the Boone and Crockett Club's® records, North American big game harvested by the use of the following methods or under the following conditions are ineligible:

I. Spotting or herding game from the air, followed by landing in its vicinity for the purpose of pursuit and shooting;
II. Herding or chasing with the aid of any motorized equipment;
III. Use of electronic communication devices to guide hunters to game, artificial lighting, electronic light intensifying devices (night vision optics), sights with built-in electronic range-finding capabilities, thermal imaging equipment, electronic game calls or cameras/timers/motion tracking devices that transmit images and other information to the hunter;
IV. Confined by artificial barriers, including escape-proof fenced enclosures;
V. Transplanted for the purpose of commercial shooting;
VI. By the use of traps or pharmaceuticals;
VII. While swimming, helpless in deep snow, or helpless in any other natural or artificial medium;
VIII. On another hunter's license;
IX. Not in full compliance with the game laws or regulations of the federal government or of any state, province, territory, or tribal council on reservations or tribal lands;

I certify that the trophy scored on this chart was not taken in violation of the conditions listed above. In signing this statement, I understand that if the information provided on this entry is found to be misrepresented or fraudulent in any respect, it will not be accepted into the Awards Program and 1) all of my prior entries are subject to deletion from future editions of **Records of North American Big Game** 2) future entries may not be accepted.

FAIR CHASE, as defined by the Boone and Crockett Club®, is the ethical, sportsmanlike and lawful pursuit and taking of any free-ranging wild, native North American big game animal in a manner that does not give the hunter an improper advantage over such game animals.

The Boone and Crockett Club® may exclude the entry of any animal that it deems to have been taken in an unethical manner or under conditions deemed inappropriate by the Club.

Date: _____ Signature of Hunter: _____
(SIGNATURE MUST BE WITNESSED BY AN OFFICIAL MEASURER OR A NOTARY PUBLIC.)

Date: _____ Signature of Notary or Official Measurer: _____

Legendary Adventures

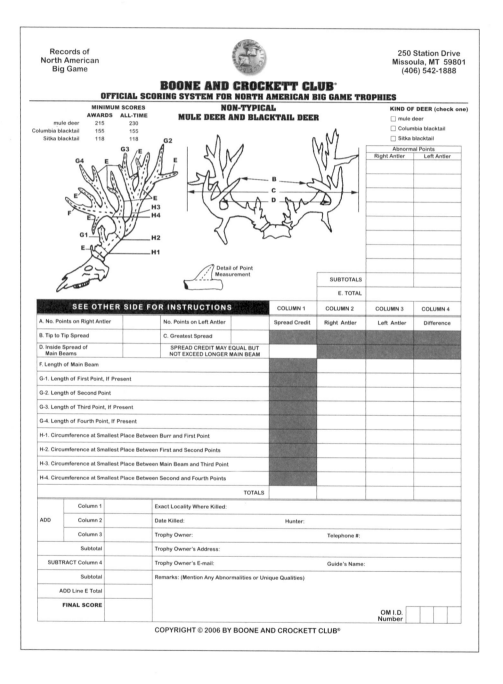

250 Station Drive
Missoula, MT 59801
(406) 542-1888

BOONE AND CROCKETT CLUB

OFFICIAL SCORING SYSTEM FOR NORTH AMERICAN BIG GAME TROPHIES

NON-TYPICAL
MULE DEER AND BLACKTAIL DEER

	MINIMUM SCORES	
	AWARDS	ALL-TIME
mule deer	215	230
Columbia blacktail	155	155
Sitka blacktail	118	118

KIND OF DEER (check one)
- [ ] mule deer
- [ ] Columbia blacktail
- [ ] Sitka blacktail

Abnormal Points	
Right Antler	Left Antler
SUBTOTALS	
E. TOTAL	

Detail of Point Measurement

SEE OTHER SIDE FOR INSTRUCTIONS		COLUMN 1	COLUMN 2	COLUMN 3	COLUMN 4
A. No. Points on Right Antler	No. Points on Left Antler	Spread Credit	Right Antler	Left Antler	Difference
B. Tip to Tip Spread	C. Greatest Spread				
D. Inside Spread of Main Beams	SPREAD CREDIT MAY EQUAL BUT NOT EXCEED LONGER MAIN BEAM				
F. Length of Main Beam					
G-1. Length of First Point, If Present					
G-2. Length of Second Point					
G-3. Length of Third Point, If Present					
G-4. Length of Fourth Point, If Present					
H-1. Circumference at Smallest Place Between Burr and First Point					
H-2. Circumference at Smallest Place Between First and Second Points					
H-3. Circumference at Smallest Place Between Main Beam and Third Point					
H-4. Circumference at Smallest Place Between Second and Fourth Points					
TOTALS					

ADD	Column 1	
	Column 2	
	Column 3	
	Subtotal	
SUBTRACT Column 4		
	Subtotal	
ADD Line E Total		
FINAL SCORE		

Exact Locality Where Killed:

Date Killed: Hunter:

Trophy Owner: Telephone #:

Trophy Owner's Address:

Trophy Owner's E-mail: Guide's Name:

Remarks: (Mention Any Abnormalities or Unique Qualities)

OM I.D.
Number

I, _____ , certify that I have measured this trophy on _____
        PRINT NAME   MM/DD/YYYY

at _____
   STREET ADDRESS   CITY   STATE/PROVINCE

and that these measurements and data are, to the best of my knowledge and belief, made in accordance with the instructions given.

Witness: _____ Signature: _____ I.D. Number [ ][ ][ ][ ]
                                                 B&C OFFICIAL MEASURER

INSTRUCTIONS FOR MEASURING NON-TYPICAL MULE DEER AND BLACKTAIL

All measurements must be made with a 1/4-inch wide flexible steel tape to the nearest one-eighth of an inch. (Note: A flexible steel cable can be used to measure points and main beams only.) Enter fractional figures in eighths, without reduction. Official measurements cannot be taken until the antlers have air dried for at least 60 days after the animal was killed.

  A. Number of Points on Each Antler: To be counted a point, the projection must be at least one inch long, with length exceeding width at one inch or more of length. All points are measured from tip of point to nearest edge of beam as illustrated. Beam tip is counted as a point but not measured as a point. **Point totals do not add into the final score.**

  B. Tip to Tip Spread is measured between tips of main beams. **Tip to tip spread does not add into the final score.**

  C. Greatest Spread is measured between perpendiculars at a right angle to the center line of the skull at widest part, whether across main beams or points. **Greatest spread does not add into the final score.**

  D. Inside Spread of Main Beams is measured at a right angle to the center line of the skull at widest point between main beams. Enter this measurement again as the Spread Credit if it is less than or equal to the length of the longer main beam; if greater, enter longer main beam length for Spread Credit.

  E. Total of Lengths of all Abnormal Points: Abnormal Points are those non-typical in location such as points originating from a point (exception: G-3 originates from G-2 in perfectly normal fashion) or from bottom or sides of main beam, or any points beyond the normal pattern of five (including beam tip) per antler. Measure each abnormal point in usual manner and enter in appropriate blanks.

  F. Length of Main Beam is measured from the center of the lowest outside edge of burr over the outer side to the most distant point of the main beam. The point of beginning is that point on the burr where the center line along the outer side of the beam intersects the burr, then following generally the line of the illustration.

  G-1-2-3-4. Length of Normal Points: Normal points are the brow tines and the upper and lower forks as shown in the illustration. They are measured from nearest edge of main beam over outer curve to tip. Lay the tape along the outer curve of the beam so that the top edge of the tape coincides with the top edge of the beam on both sides of point to determine the baseline for point measurement. Record point lengths in appropriate blanks.

  H-1-2-3-4. Circumferences are taken as detailed in illustration for each measurement. If brow point is missing, take H-1 and H-2 at smallest place between burr and G-2. If G-3 is missing, take H-3 halfway between the base and tip of G-2. If G-4 is missing, take H-4 halfway between G-2 and tip of main beam.

ENTRY AFFIDAVIT FOR ALL HUNTER-TAKEN TROPHIES

For the purpose of entry into the Boone and Crockett Club's® records, North American big game harvested by the use of the following methods or under the following conditions are ineligible:

  I.   Spotting or herding game from the air, followed by landing in its vicinity for the purpose of pursuit and shooting;
  II. Herding or chasing with the aid of any motorized equipment;
  III. Use of electronic communication devices to guide hunters to game, artificial lighting, electronic light intensifying devices (night vision optics), sights with built-in electronic range-finding capabilities, thermal imaging equipment, electronic game calls or cameras/timers/motion tracking devices that transmit images and other information to the hunter;
  IV. Confined by artificial barriers, including escape-proof fenced enclosures;
  V. Transplanted for the purpose of commercial shooting;
  VI. By the use of traps or pharmaceuticals;
  VII. While swimming, helpless in deep snow, or helpless in any other natural or artificial medium;
  VIII. On another hunter's license;
  IX. Not in full compliance with the game laws or regulations of the federal government or of any state, province, territory, or tribal council on reservations or tribal lands;

I certify that the trophy scored on this chart was not taken in violation of the conditions listed above. In signing this statement, I understand that if the information provided on this entry is found to be misrepresented or fraudulent in any respect, it will not be accepted into the Awards Program and 1) all of my prior entries are subject to deletion from future editions of **Records of North American Big Game** 2) future entries may not be accepted.

FAIR CHASE, as defined by the Boone and Crockett Club®, is the ethical, sportsmanlike and lawful pursuit and taking of any free-ranging wild, native North American big game animal in a manner that does not give the hunter an improper advantage over such game animals.

The Boone and Crockett Club® may exclude the entry of any animal that it deems to have been taken in an unethical manner or under conditions deemed inappropriate by the Club.

Date: _____ Signature of Hunter: _____
                                       (SIGNATURE MUST BE WITNESSED BY AN OFFICIAL MEASURER OR A NOTARY PUBLIC.)

Date: _____ Signature of Notary or Official Measurer: _____

Legendary Adventures

250 Station Drive
Missoula, MT 59801
(406) 542-1888

BOONE AND CROCKETT CLUB®
OFFICIAL SCORING SYSTEM FOR NORTH AMERICAN BIG GAME TROPHIES

MINIMUM SCORES

	AWARDS	ALL-TIME
whitetail	160	170
Coues'	100	110

TYPICAL
WHITETAIL AND COUES' DEER

KIND OF DEER (check one)
☐ whitetail
☐ Coues'

Detail of Point Measurement

	Abnormal Points	
	Right Antler	Left Antler
SUBTOTALS		
TOTAL TO E		

SEE OTHER SIDE FOR INSTRUCTIONS

			COLUMN 1	COLUMN 2	COLUMN 3	COLUMN 4
A. No. Points on Right Antler		No. Points on Left Antler	Spread Credit	Right Antler	Left Antler	Difference
B. Tip to Tip Spread		C. Greatest Spread				
D. Inside Spread of Main Beams		SPREAD CREDIT MAY EQUAL BUT NOT EXCEED LONGER MAIN BEAM				
E. Total of Lengths of Abnormal Points						
F. Length of Main Beam						
G-1. Length of First Point						
G-2. Length of Second Point						
G-3. Length of Third Point						
G-4. Length of Fourth Point, If Present						
G-5. Length of Fifth Point, If Present						
G-6. Length of Sixth Point, If Present						
G-7. Length of Seventh Point, If Present						
H-1. Circumference at Smallest Place Between Burr and First Point						
H-2. Circumference at Smallest Place Between First and Second Points						
H-3. Circumference at Smallest Place Between Second and Third Points						
H-4. Circumference at Smallest Place Between Third and Fourth Points						
		TOTALS				

ADD	Column 1		Exact Locality Where Killed:	
	Column 2		Date Killed:	Hunter:
	Column 3		Trophy Owner:	Telephone #:
	Subtotal		Trophy Owner's Address:	
SUBTRACT Column 4			Trophy Owner's E-mail:	Guide's Name:
FINAL SCORE			Remarks: (Mention Any Abnormalities or Unique Qualities)	OM I.D. Number

202

I, _____ , certify that I have measured this trophy on _____
PRINT NAME   MM/DD/YYYYY

at _____   _____   _____
STREET ADDRESS   CITY   STATE/PROVINCE

and that these measurements and data are, to the best of my knowledge and belief, made in accordance with the instructions given.

Witness: _____ Signature: _____ I.D. Number ☐ ☐ ☐ ☐
                                               B&C OFFICIAL MEASURER

INSTRUCTIONS FOR MEASURING TYPICAL WHITETAIL AND COUES' DEER

All measurements must be made with a 1/4-inch wide flexible steel tape to the nearest one-eighth of an inch. (Note: A flexible steel cable can be used to measure points and main beams only.) Enter fractional figures in eighths, without reduction. Official measurements cannot be taken until the antlers have air dried for at least 60 days after the animal was killed.

A. Number of Points on Each Antler: To be counted a point, the projection must be at least one inch long, with the length exceeding width at one inch or more of length. All points are measured from tip of point to nearest edge of beam as illustrated. Beam tip is counted as a point but not measured as a point. **Point totals do not add into the final score.**

B. Tip to Tip Spread is measured between tips of main beams. **Tip to tip spread does not add into the final score.**

C. Greatest Spread is measured between perpendiculars at a right angle to the center line of the skull at widest part, whether across main beams or points. **Greatest spread does not add into the final score.**

D. Inside Spread of Main Beams is measured at a right angle to the center line of the skull at widest point between main beams. Enter this measurement again as the Spread Credit if it is less than or equal to the length of the longer main beam; if greater, enter longer main beam length for Spread Credit.

E. Total of Lengths of all Abnormal Points: Abnormal Points are those non-typical in location (such as points originating from a point or from bottom or sides of main beam) or extra points beyond the normal pattern of points. Measure in usual manner and enter in appropriate blanks.

F. Length of Main Beam is measured from the center of the lowest outside edge of burr over the outer side to the most distant point of the main beam. The point of beginning is that point on the burr where the center line along the outer side of the beam intersects the burr, then following generally the line of the illustration.

G-1-2-3-4-5-6-7. Length of Normal Points: Normal points project from the top of the main beam. They are measured from nearest edge of main beam over outer curve to tip. Lay the tape along the outer curve of the beam so that the top edge of the tape coincides with the top edge of the beam on both sides of the point to determine the baseline for point measurements. Record point lengths in appropriate blanks.

H-1-2-3-4. Circumferences are taken as detailed in illustration for each measurement. If brow point is missing, take H-1 and H-2 at smallest place between burr and G-2. If G-4 is missing, take H-4 halfway between G-3 and tip of main beam.

ENTRY AFFIDAVIT FOR ALL HUNTER-TAKEN TROPHIES

For the purpose of entry into the Boone and Crockett Club's® records, North American big game harvested by the use of the following methods or under the following conditions are ineligible:

I.   Spotting or herding game from the air, followed by landing in its vicinity for the purpose of pursuit and shooting;
II. Herding or chasing with the aid of any motorized equipment;
III. Use of electronic communication devices to guide hunters to game, artificial lighting, electronic light intensifying devices (night vision optics), sights with built-in electronic range-finding capabilities, thermal imaging equipment, electronic game calls or cameras/timers/motion tracking devices that transmit images and other information to the hunter;
IV. Confined by artificial barriers, including escape-proof fenced enclosures;
V.   Transplanted for the purpose of commercial shooting;
VI. By the use of traps or pharmaceuticals;
VII. While swimming, helpless in deep snow, or helpless in any other natural or artificial medium;
VIII. On another hunter's license;
IX. Not in full compliance with the game laws or regulations of the federal government or of any state, province, territory, or tribal council on reservations or tribal lands;

I certify that the trophy scored on this chart was not taken in violation of the conditions listed above. In signing this statement, I understand that if the information provided on this entry is found to be misrepresented or fraudulent in any respect, it will not be accepted into the Awards Program and 1) all of my prior entries are subject to deletion from future editions of **Records of North American Big Game** 2) future entries may not be accepted.

FAIR CHASE, as defined by the Boone and Crockett Club®, is the ethical, sportsmanlike and lawful pursuit and taking of any free-ranging wild, native North American big game animal in a manner that does not give the hunter an improper advantage over such game animals.

The Boone and Crockett Club® may exclude the entry of any animal that it deems to have been taken in an unethical manner or under conditions deemed inappropriate by the Club.

Date: _____ Signature of Hunter: _____
                                          (SIGNATURE MUST BE WITNESSED BY AN OFFICIAL MEASURER OR A NOTARY PUBLIC.)

Date: _____ Signature of Notary or Official Measurer: _____

Records of
North American
Big Game

250 Station Drive
Missoula, MT 59801
(406) 542-1888

BOONE AND CROCKETT CLUB®
OFFICIAL SCORING SYSTEM FOR NORTH AMERICAN BIG GAME TROPHIES

NON-TYPICAL
WHITETAIL AND COUES' DEER

MINIMUM SCORES	AWARDS	ALL-TIME
whitetail	185	195
Coues'	105	120

KIND OF DEER (check one)
☐ whitetail
☐ Coues'

Abnormal Points	
Right Antler	Left Antler
SUBTOTALS	
E. TOTAL	

Detail of Point
Measurement

SEE OTHER SIDE FOR INSTRUCTIONS		COLUMN 1	COLUMN 2	COLUMN 3	COLUMN 4
A. No. Points on Right Antler	No. Points on Left Antler	Spread Credit	Right Antler	Left Antler	Difference
B. Tip to Tip Spread	C. Greatest Spread				
D. Inside Spread of Main Beams	SPREAD CREDIT MAY EQUAL BUT NOT EXCEED LONGER MAIN BEAM				
F. Length of Main Beam					
G-1. Length of First Point					
G-2. Length of Second Point					
G-3. Length of Third Point					
G-4. Length of Fourth Point, If Present					
G-5. Length of Fifth Point, If Present					
G-6. Length of Sixth Point, If Present					
G-7. Length of Seventh Point, If Present					
H-1. Circumference at Smallest Place Between Burr and First Point					
H-2. Circumference at Smallest Place Between First and Second Points					
H-3. Circumference at Smallest Place Between Second and Third Points					
H-4. Circumference at Smallest Place Between Third and Fourth Points					
TOTALS					

ADD	Column 1	
	Column 2	
	Column 3	
	Subtotal	
SUBTRACT Column 4		
	Subtotal	
	ADD Line E Total	
FINAL SCORE		

Exact Locality Where Killed:

Date Killed: Hunter:

Trophy Owner: Telephone #:

Trophy Owner's Address:

Trophy Owner's E-mail: Guide's Name:

Remarks: (Mention Any Abnormalities or Unique Qualities)

OM I.D.
Number

I, _____ , certify that I have measured this trophy on _____
PRINT NAME   MM/DD/YYYYY

at _____ _____ _____
STREET ADDRESS   CITY   STATE/PROVINCE

and that these measurements and data are, to the best of my knowledge and belief, made in accordance with the instructions given.

Witness: _____ Signature: _____ I.D. Number
                                           B&C OFFICIAL MEASURER

INSTRUCTIONS FOR MEASURING NON-TYPICAL WHITETAIL AND COUES' DEER

All measurements must be made with a 1/4-inch wide flexible steel tape to the nearest one-eighth of an inch. (Note: A flexible steel cable can be used to measure points and main beams only.) Enter fractional figures in eighths, without reduction. Official measurements cannot be taken until the antlers have air dried for at least 60 days after the animal was killed.

A. Number of Points on Each Antler: To be counted a point, the projection must be at least one inch long, with the length exceeding width at one inch or more of length. All points are measured from tip of point to nearest edge of beam as illustrated. Beam tip is counted as a point but not measured as a point. **Point totals do not add into the final score.**

B. Tip to Tip Spread is measured between tips of main beams. **Tip to tip spread does not add into the final score.**

C. Greatest Spread is measured between perpendiculars at a right angle to the center line of the skull at widest part, whether across main beams or points. **Greatest spread does not add into the final score.**

D. Inside Spread of Main Beams is measured at a right angle to the center line of the skull at widest point between main beams. Enter this measurement again as the Spread Credit if it is less than or equal to the length of the longer main beam; if greater, enter longer main beam length for Spread Credit.

E. Total of Lengths of all Abnormal Points: Abnormal Points are those non-typical in location (such as points originating from a point or from bottom or sides of main beam) or extra points beyond the normal pattern of points. Measure in usual manner and enter in appropriate blanks.

F. Length of Main Beam is measured from the center of the lowest outside edge of burr over the outer side to the most distant point of the main beam. The point of beginning is that point on the burr where the center line along the outer side of the beam intersects the burr, then following generally the line of the illustration.

G-1-2-3-4-5-6-7. Length of Normal Points: Normal points project from the top of the main beam. They are measured from nearest edge of main beam over outer curve to tip. Lay the tape along the outer curve of the beam so that the top edge of the tape coincides with the top edge of the beam on both sides of the point to determine the baseline for point measurement. Record point lengths in appropriate blanks.

H-1-2-3-4. Circumferences are taken as detailed in illustration for each measurement. If brow point is missing, take H-1 and H-2 at smallest place between burr and G-2. If G-4 is missing, take H-4 halfway between G-3 and tip of main beam.

ENTRY AFFIDAVIT FOR ALL HUNTER-TAKEN TROPHIES

For the purpose of entry into the Boone and Crockett Club's® records, North American big game harvested by the use of the following methods or under the following conditions are ineligible:

I.   Spotting or herding game from the air, followed by landing in its vicinity for the purpose of pursuit and shooting;
II. Herding or chasing with the aid of any motorized equipment;
III. Use of electronic communication devices to guide hunters to game, artificial lighting, electronic light intensifying devices (night vision optics), sights with built-in electronic range-finding capabilities, thermal imaging equipment, electronic game calls or cameras/timers/motion tracking devices that transmit images and other information to the hunter;
IV. Confined by artificial barriers, including escape-proof fenced enclosures;
V.   Transplanted for the purpose of commercial shooting;
VI. By the use of traps or pharmaceuticals;
VII. While swimming, helpless in deep snow, or helpless in any other natural or artificial medium;
VIII. On another hunter's license;
IX. Not in full compliance with the game laws or regulations of the federal government or of any state, province, territory, or tribal council on reservations or tribal lands;

I certify that the trophy scored on this chart was not taken in violation of the conditions listed above. In signing this statement, I understand that if the information provided on this entry is found to be misrepresented or fraudulent in any respect, it will not be accepted into the Awards Program and 1) all of my prior entries are subject to deletion from future editions of **Records of North American Big Game** 2) future entries may not be accepted.

FAIR CHASE, as defined by the Boone and Crockett Club®, is the ethical, sportsmanlike and lawful pursuit and taking of any free-ranging wild, native North American big game animal in a manner that does not give the hunter an improper advantage over such game animals.

The Boone and Crockett Club® may exclude the entry of any animal that it deems to have been taken in an unethical manner or under conditions deemed inappropriate by the Club.

Date: _____ Signature of Hunter: _____
                                         (SIGNATURE MUST BE WITNESSED BY AN OFFICIAL MEASURER OR A NOTARY PUBLIC.)

Date: _____ Signature of Notary or Official Measurer: _____

Legendary Adventures

BOONE AND CROCKETT CLUB®
OFFICIAL SCORING SYSTEM FOR NORTH AMERICAN BIG GAME TROPHIES
PRONGHORN

MINIMUM SCORES	
AWARDS	ALL-TIME
80	82

SEE OTHER SIDE FOR INSTRUCTIONS		COLUMN 1	COLUMN 2	COLUMN 3
A. Tip to Tip Spread		Right	Left	
B. Inside Spread of Horns		Horn	Horn	Difference
C. Length of Horn				
D-1. Circumference of Base				
D-2. Circumference at First Quarter	Location of First Quarter Circumference: _____			
D-3. Circumference at Second Quarter	Location of Second Quarter Circumference: _____			
D-4. Circumference at Third Quarter	Location of Third Quarter Circumference: _____			
E. Length of Prong				
	TOTALS			

ADD	Column 1		Exact Locality Where Killed:
	Column 2		Date Killed: Hunter:
	Subtotal		Trophy Owner: Telephone #:
	SUBTRACT Column 3		Trophy Owner's Address:
FINAL SCORE			Trophy Owner's E-mail: Guide's Name:
			Remarks: (Mention Any Abnormalities or Unique Qualities)

At the time of official measurement, were the sheaths reattached to the cores by the use of some type of filler or adhesive? ☐Yes ☐No

I, _____ , certify that I have measured this trophy on _____
　　　　PRINT NAME　　　　　　　　　　　　　　　　　　　　　　　　　　　　MM/DD/YYYY

at _____
　　STREET ADDRESS　　　　　　　　　　　　　　　　CITY　　　　　　　STATE/PROVINCE

and that these measurements and data are, to the best of my knowledge and belief, made in accordance with the instructions given.

Witness: _____ Signature: _____ I.D. Number [ ][ ][ ]
　　　　　　　　　　　　　　　　　　　　　　　B&C OFFICIAL MEASURER

INSTRUCTIONS FOR MEASURING PRONGHORN

All measurements must be made with a 1/4-inch wide flexible steel tape to the nearest one-eighth of an inch. Enter fractional figures in eighths, without reduction. Official measurements cannot be taken until horns have air dried for at least 60 days after the animal was killed.

    A. Tip to Tip Spread is measured between tips of horns. **Tip to tip spread does not add into the final score.**

    B. Inside Spread of Horns is measured at a right angle to the center line of the skull, at widest point between horns. **Inside spread does not add into the final score.**

    C. Length of Horn is measured on the outside curve on the general line illustrated. The line taken will vary with different heads, depending on the direction of their curvature. Measure along the center of the outer curve from tip of horn to a point in line with the lowest edge of the base, using a straight edge to establish the line end.

    D-1. Circumference of Base is measured at a right angle to axis of horn. Do not follow irregular edge of horn; the line of measurement must be entirely on horn material.

    D-2-3-4. Divide measurement C of longer horn by four. Starting at base, mark both horns at these quarters (even though the other horn is shorter) and measure circumferences at these marks. If the prong interferes with D-2, move the measurement down to just below the swelling of the prong. If D-3 falls in the swelling of the prong, move the measurement up to just above the prong.

    E. Length of Prong: Measure from the tip of the prong along the upper edge of the outer side to the horn; then continue around the horn to a point at the rear of the horn where a straight edge across the back of both horns touches the horn, with the latter part being at a right angle to the long axis of horn.

ENTRY AFFIDAVIT FOR ALL HUNTER-TAKEN TROPHIES

For the purpose of entry into the Boone and Crockett Club's® records, North American big game harvested by the use of the following methods or under the following conditions are ineligible:

    I. Spotting or herding game from the air, followed by landing in its vicinity for the purpose of pursuit and shooting;

    II. Herding or chasing with the aid of any motorized equipment;

    III. Use of electronic communication devices to guide hunters to game, artificial lighting, electronic light intensifying devices (night vision optics), sights with built-in electronic range-finding capabilities, thermal imaging equipment, electronic game calls or cameras/timers/motion tracking devices that transmit images and other information to the hunter;

    IV. Confined by artificial barriers, including escape-proof fenced enclosures;

    V. Transplanted for the purpose of commercial shooting;

    VI. By the use of traps or pharmaceuticals;

    VII. While swimming, helpless in deep snow, or helpless in any other natural or artificial medium;

    VIII. On another hunter's license;

    IX. Not in full compliance with the game laws or regulations of the federal government or of any state, province, territory, or tribal council on reservations or tribal lands;

I certify that the trophy scored on this chart was not taken in violation of the conditions listed above. In signing this statement, I understand that if the information provided on this entry is found to be misrepresented or fraudulent in any respect, it will not be accepted into the Awards Program and 1) all of my prior entries are subject to deletion from future editions of **Records of North American Big Game** 2) future entries may not be accepted.

FAIR CHASE, as defined by the Boone and Crockett Club®, is the ethical, sportsmanlike and lawful pursuit and taking of any free-ranging wild, native North American big game animal in a manner that does not give the hunter an improper advantage over such game animals.

The Boone and Crockett Club® may exclude the entry of any animal that it deems to have been taken in an unethical manner or under conditions deemed inappropriate by the Club.

Date: _____ Signature of Hunter: _____
                                                 (SIGNATURE MUST BE WITNESSED BY AN OFFICIAL MEASURER OR A NOTARY PUBLIC.)

Date: _____ Signature of Notary or Official Measurer: _____

Legendary Adventures
Hunter's Equipment Checklist

Clothing
- ❏ Socks
- ❏ Long underwear (like "Polartec")
- ❏ Shirts (long and short sleeved)
- ❏ Hat or cap
- ❏ Jacket (one heavy, one light)
- ❏ Handkerchiefs
- ❏ Underwear
- ❏ Pants
- ❏ Gloves
- ❏ Rain gear (top and bottom)
- ❏ Fleece vest
- ❏ Travel clothes (to and from camp)

Footwear
- ❏ Boots (2 pairs)
- ❏ Gore-tex or wool socks
- ❏ Camp shoes (lightweight hiking)
- ❏ Blister kit (moleskin)

Sleeping
- ❏ Sleeping bag (mummy style)
- ❏ Pillow
- ❏ Waterproof stuff sack
- ❏ Bed roll

Hunting Gear
- ❏ Frame pack
- ❏ Binoculars
- ❏ Hunting knife
- ❏ Rifle hunters
- ❏ Scope covers
- ❏ Cleaning kit
- ❏ Hard gun case
- ❏ Day pack
- ❏ Lens cleaner/cloth
- ❏ Knife sharpener
- ❏ Gun and scope
- ❏ Ammunition (1 or 2 boxes?)
- ❏ Oil (or rust preventer)

Bow Hunters

- ❑ Box
- ❑ Releases (mechanical or tab)
- ❑ Arm guard
- ❑ Bludgeon (judo point)
- ❑ Quiver
- ❑ String wax
- ❑ Extra string
- ❑ Bow sling
- ❑ Arrows (1 to 2 dozen)
- ❑ Broadheads
- ❑ Wrenches

Muzzleloader Hunters

- ❑ Gun
- ❑ Pellets or powder
- ❑ Quickloaders
- ❑ Cleaning rod
- ❑ Breech plug grease
- ❑ Old toothbrush
- ❑ Twenty 300 gr. bullets (your call)
- ❑ Caps or 209 primers
- ❑ Breech tool
- ❑ Bullet puller
- ❑ Cleaning patches

Miscellaneous

- ❑ Camera
- ❑ Water bottle
- ❑ Bug repellent
- ❑ Hunting and fishing licenses
- ❑ Hunter's education card (*a must*)
- ❑ Flashlight (with batteries)
- ❑ Matches, butane lighter
- ❑ Compass
- ❑ Passport, wallet, credit card, and ID

Personal

- ❑ Toothbrush, toothpaste
- ❑ Chap stick
- ❑ Glasses or contacts
- ❑ Band-Aids (First aid)
- ❑ Scent-free soap
- ❑ Deodorant
- ❑ Painkillers (pills)
- ❑ Razor

Optional

- ❑ Spotting scope
- ❑ Range finder
- ❑ Gators for snakes
- ❑ Safety blanket
- ❑ Athlete's foot cream
- ❑ Tripod
- ❑ Fishing pole
- ❑ Face paint
- ❑ Water filter
- ❑ Small notepad and pen